JOHN P. CAVES III

The New Model Federalist

A Series of Essays on the Political Situation of the United States

Copyright © 2021 by John P. Caves III

All rights reserved. No part of this publication may be reproduced, stored or transmitted in any form or by any means, electronic, mechanical, photocopying, recording, scanning, or otherwise without written permission from the publisher. It is illegal to copy this book, post it to a website, or distribute it by any other means without permission.

This is the first paperback edition of this work. The essays comprising the main body of this work were first published by the author in 2019 and 2020 at https://newmodelfederalist.net.

First edition

ISBN: 978-1-7369245-2-5

Cover art by Diana DiGasbarro

This book was professionally typeset on Reedsy. Find out more at reedsy.com

Contents

Foreword	iv
The New Model Federalist	1
The Situation of These United States	3
No. 1 – On Fundamental Liberties	8
No. 2 – On Federalism	18
No. 3 – On Representative Government	34
No. 4 – On Bureaucracy	46
No. 5 – On the National Debt	57
No. 6 – On Entitlements	68
No. 7 – On Economic Inequality	84
No. 8 – On Trade	100
No. 9 – On Citizenship	114
No. 10 – On Immigration	127
No. 11 – On Foreign Policy	141
No. 12 – On International Cooperation	159
No. 13 – On Great Works	172
The Past, The Present, and The Future	186
Afterword	191
Acknowledgments	199
Bibliography	201
About the Author	206
Notes	207

Foreword

February 13th, 2021

In 1852, Frederick Douglass said: "I hold that every American citizen has a right to form an opinion of the Constitution, and to propagate that opinion, and to use all honorable means to make his opinion the prevailing one."[1]

The 2016 election spurred me to exercise that right by writing a series of essays about the classical principles that the United States was founded upon and how we could apply them to our Republic's challenges today. I first published them between September 2019 and March 2020 on a website I created for that purpose, newmodelfederalist.net.

I see these essays as having two purposes.

First, to tug our national conversation back toward our founding principles. There are, to be sure, plenty of ideas in these essays, as in any political writing, that could prove over time to be misguided. But if they can help simply to get us thinking and talking more about what our guiding principles are or ought to be, and how the most longstanding principles should be interpreted, then I think they will have done a clear good.

Second, to contribute to an intellectual basis for a new political party, or a reforming faction within either the burnt shell of the Republican Party or the centrist edge of the Democratic Party, that is built around classical liberalism, federalism, sensible free-market economics, and the preservation of the United States as a powerful force for liberty in the world. This is an ambitious goal, and I am keenly aware both that it cannot be done by one person alone and that its time may not yet have come. Yet I have something to offer now, and so I am offering it.

In preparation for writing these essays, I read, or re-read, the Constitution, the Federalist Papers, and other works by our U.S. Founders and several of the Enlightenment thinkers who influenced them—from John Locke and Montesquieu to Adam Smith and Edmund Burke—as well as works by 19th and early 20th century figures who observed what the Founders made or carried their torch: Alexis de Tocqueville, Frederick Douglass, and Theodore Roosevelt, to name a few. I draw less from more recent thinkers, not because their work does not have great value, but because I saw value in looking back to the beginning and trying to understand what those historic figures thought without the lens of intermediary interpretations. Excerpts from their writings and speeches are contained in the notes, which are meant to be read along with the main body of the essays.

I self-published this work, rather than approach a traditional publisher, because it is of a genre and format common to the 17th and 18th centuries but unusual for our time: the political pamphlet or essay series, the most famous of which are the Federalist Papers. Unlike chapters of a book, each essay can stand alone; but unlike newspaper opinion articles, they are meant as a set and are better understood if read together and sequentially. They are neither academic nor lawyerly nor casual. They are meant to be read thoughtfully, but do not require specialized education to be understood.

I did, however, make a deliberate decision to write the essays in a style echoing that which our Republic's Founders used in their writing (while omitting such difficult-to-read aspects as the capitalization of every noun or certain uses of commas that are no longer familiar to us). I did so to evoke the cadence of our founding documents, and also because I feel that we as a nation could benefit by restoring some dignity to our discussion of politics. Eighteenth-century political writing, or at least those products of it that have stood the test of time, was distinctly high-minded and dignified in tone compared to much of what we read today.

Where these essays reference recent events, they are largely the happenings of 2016-2019, which is the period when I did most of my writing and refining. Only the postscript, finished on March 29, 2020, reckons with that year's defining occurrence: the COVID-19 pandemic. Overall, the essays may be seen as a window looking out onto the troubled waning years of the 21st century's second decade, on whose horizon emerges the momentous events of 2020.

The momentous events that happened beyond the view of these essays include, of course, the long summer of protest, rioting, and reprisals that followed the unjust killing of Mr. George Floyd; the massive and rising toll of COVID-19, which at the time of this writing exceeds 400,000 American lives; the insidious attempt by Donald Trump to cling unlawfully to power by casting false doubt on the election he lost, which culminated in the violent attempt on the Capitol of January 6th, 2021; and the subsequent failure of Congress to convict him in a trial of impeachment. Rather than render this work obsolete, those events have shown, in stark terms, the importance of the principles and the urgency of the warnings contained within them.

Some other events have also transpired that bear on the subjects discussed in these essays. The several-trillion-dollar increase to the public debt in response to Covid-19, while unavoidable, was an example of the type of unforeseen event described in the fifth essay, on the national debt. Federal anti-trust lawsuits have been brought against Facebook and Google in tandem with multiple Congressional hearings on the subject, which portends bipartisan movement on the issue of competition discussed in the seventh essay, on economic inequality. In a referendum concurrent with the general election in November, the residents of Puerto Rico voted in favor of statehood, an issue discussed in the ninth essay, on citizenship. Hearteningly, in a year that brought little good news, NASA and SpaceX transported American astronauts safely to and from the International Space Station, heralding the success of NASA's Commercial Crew Program and ending a nine-year reliance on Russia's space agency, a subject discussed in the thirteenth essay, on the great works of conservation and exploration.

None of the challenges now facing our Republic, however, have so far been put to rest. I hope only that, in reading these essays, you encounter one more perspective that constructively contributes to the great and ongoing debate about how we as citizens may form a more perfect Union, and so secure the blessings of liberty to ourselves and our posterity.

—John P. Caves III

Note: As the main body of this work (excluding the Foreword and Afterword) was written between 2016 and 2020, references made to "the present administration" refer to the Trump administration, and references to "the previous administration" refer to the Obama administration.

The New Model Federalist

A Series of Essays
Concerning
The Political Situation of These United States of America
Which
Draw Upon the Founding Principles of Our Union
In Order To
Propose a New Way Forward
So That
This Republic Shall Sustain Its Might and Liberty Throughout the 21st Century

Composed with the advice and feedback of several fellow Americans
And
Dedicated to those generations of citizens who have maintained the Republic before us
It is hereby
Respectfully submitted to the public for consideration

"Thus, it is very likely that ultimately men would have been obliged to live forever under the government of one alone if they had not devised a kind of constitution that has all the internal advantages of republican government and the external force of monarchy. I speak of the federal republic." —Charles de Secondat, Baron Montesquieu, 1748. *The Spirit of the Laws*, Bk. 9, Ch. 1.

"It is rather for us to be here dedicated to the great task remaining before us – that from these honored dead we take increased devotion to that cause for which they gave the last full measure of devotion – that we here highly resolve that these dead shall not have died in vain – that this nation, under God, shall have a new birth of freedom – and that government of the people, by the people, for the people, shall not perish from the earth." —Abraham Lincoln, November 19th, 1863. *Gettysburg Address*.

The Situation of These United States

> "After an unequivocal experience of the inefficacy of the subsisting Federal Government, you are called upon to deliberate on a new Constitution for the United States of America. The subject speaks its own importance; comprehending in its consequences, nothing less than the existence of the Union, the safety and welfare of the parts of which it is composed, the fate of an empire, in many respects, the most interesting in the world." —**Alexander Hamilton, *Federalist No. 1*, October 27th, 1787.**

At the close of the 17th century, the West began to build its political edifice upon the foundation of the Enlightenment, and from that time on free societies have been able to persevere around the world. The United States of America, with its Declaration of Independence in 1776 and its Constitution in 1787, was the first country designed deliberately to be governed according to Enlightenment principles, and has to show for it two-hundred and forty-three years of largely prosperous and victorious history. Yet these principles and the freedom they bestow have from time to time been threatened:

by slavery and absolutism in the 18th and 19th centuries; by fascism and communism in the 20th; and in the 21st by the insidious proponents of 'illiberal democracy.'

Illiberal democracy, a term coined derisively by the theorist Fareed Zakaria but which is favored today by the despots of Eastern Europe, is the false notion that a republic can exist as such merely by holding elections; that a majority,[2] having once cast their vote for a leader, thus empowers him to suppress views he deems offensive to them; that the elected leader may, in the name of his own interpretation of the people's will, repress the political rights of the dissenting minority; and that he may push aside all constraints of law and precedent that might otherwise prevent him from carrying out his self-defined mandate.

Yet illiberal democracy is devoid of the enlightened ideas that are the cornerstones of a republic: freedom of speech, religion, assembly, and the press; the right to a fair trial; protection from self-incrimination or unwarranted search and seizure; consent of the governed; separation of powers; checks and balances; respect for property; and the inalienable rights of life, liberty, and the pursuit of happiness. Remove those founding stones, and the tower collapses. A true republic, governed by the precepts of classically liberal statecraft, serves before all other ends to preserve freedom. It holds elections not to choose a king, but because so many years of experience have proven that democracy is the best means of upholding liberty.

Challenges to this basis of free society are challenges to Western civilization itself and all the more so to these United States, which pride themselves on their freedom. Illiberal democracy is the tyranny of the majority; it is elective dictatorship; it is without liberty; it is not free.[3] Both the Republican and Democratic Parties, though to differing degrees, have failed to fully repudiate its siren call, which has sounded so loudly in recent years. The Founders of our Republic would not tolerate such inaction; nor would the philosophers who inspired them; and nor ought those who love our country and its founding principles. For if liberty cannot hold firm in these United States, the mightiest nation in the world, then it shall have no bastion anywhere. Thus must a free people take up the mantle of free government and oppose those who would undermine it.

Our Republic has become torn between notions of 'conservative' and 'liberal.' Yet those words have been perverted over decades, masking the truth that those two guiding lights lead to a destination one and the same. 'Liberal' is now an epithet for political leftism, but in its classical sense it defines a yearning for freedom, for a society free of compulsion, in which each citizen may do as he or she pleases, so long as that action does not harm the public good, stringently defined. 'Conservative' is today associated with the political right, but in its true sense it defines a wish to preserve the achievements and customs of the past.

We – defined henceforth as the author and all of those who might read these works and find them convincing – reject the modern falsifications of those words, and dare say that, as our Republic was established on classically liberal principles, to be conservative in these United States is to be liberal, and to be liberal is to be conservative. This Union cannot conserve its traditions without conserving the liberal ideals upon which it was founded; nor can it raise those ideals higher by demolishing the pillars of its heritage.

The citizens who drafted and advocated the U.S. Constitution were known as Federalists. George Washington was foremost among them. Alexander Hamilton, James Madison, and John Jay together wrote the Federalist Papers – the public explanation and defense of the Constitution by those who designed it. They had disagreements, but all strived to build a more perfect Union according to a federal plan and upon an enlightened foundation. We share those convictions, and are confident that they still can and ought to be applied to the United States in the 21st century, and that these United States can and ought to protect and perpetuate them in the wider world.

To those ends, we call for a vigorous defense of the freedoms enshrined in the First Amendment to the U.S. Constitution; limited and decentralized government in the spirit of that Constitution, which made a federal union of partly-sovereign States; the exercise of representative democracy as befits a Republic; accountability of bureaucratic agencies to elected legislatures; moderation of the public debt; return of revenue to the States, with responsibility for spending it; extension of economic opportunity through competition and investment; free trade; expansion of the Union through representation for U.S. territories; a welcome to immigrants, provided they accept the responsibility of citizenship; credible use of U.S. might in foreign affairs; reform of international institutions to attain common aims; the halt and reversal of global warming; and human space exploration leading to the spread of mankind's civilization beyond the confines of Earth. We believe these goals to be compatible, reinforcing, and, in time, achievable. We shall expound on each in its own essay, wherein we examine the principles underlying it, convey our vision of what ought to be, and propose a few broad actions which may set our Union on that path.

We, too, call ourselves Federalists, because our Republic is at its best when governed according to its federal design. Yet we also look to others, such as Democratic Republicans, Whigs, Democrats, and Republicans, for ideas that two-and-a-half centuries of experience have shown to be wise. Our goal is balance; we do not seek to push our nation interminably towards some ideological extreme of left or right. This Republic has suffered enough from that. We seek a more perfect Union, well-situated on Enlightenment principles: free, tolerant, and open, yet serious about the responsibility of citizenship, confident in the value of liberty, and sure of these United States' unique obligation and ability to defend it. Thus we ask you, fellow citizen, to read our argument from start to finish, and then make your own judgment of it.

—John P. Caves III, author, but above all, a humble Citizen

No. 1 – On Fundamental Liberties

We propose, in summary: That the rights guaranteed by the First Amendment are the foundation of free government – That speech ought not to be restricted, even if it causes offense – That the press ought to be protected, even when it is flawed – That peaceful protests ought neither to be derided by public officials nor suppressed – That there ought to be no compulsion in matters of faith – That citizens are the final guardians of First Amendment rights

> "Congress shall make no law respecting an establishment of religion, or prohibiting the free exercise thereof; or abridging the freedom of speech, or of the press; or the right of the people peaceably to assemble, and to petition the Government for a redress of grievances." —**First Amendment to the U.S. Constitution, ratified December 15th, 1791.**

To begin this series on the preservation, perpetuation, and expansion of free government in these United States and the world, we must start with free government's foundation. It consists of several pillars that stand in the way of tyranny, both of one man and of the majority, and that distinguish a republic that is free from one that merely pretends to be free

– that is, a classically liberal democracy from the 'illiberal democracy' envisioned by the would-be despots of today. These pillars were inscribed, with elegance and clarity, into the First Amendment to the U.S. Constitution. They are freedom of speech, freedom of religion, freedom of the press, and freedom of peaceable assembly. Yet the First Amendment has lately been neglected in our public debates; it is the provision of the Constitution most threatened by the proponents of illiberal democracy on both the right and left, whom the Republican and Democratic parties have been unwilling or unable to wholly disavow. Thus, it falls instead to all citizens who care for the future of their Republic to uphold its founding freedoms. We must all of us adopt the spirit of Voltaire, that "I may disagree with what you say, but I will defend to the death your right to say it."[4]

Free government – a mode of political organization in which individual citizens may live their lives peacefully and according to their preferences without government coercion, hold their own distinct opinions on public matters, and, together with their compatriots, choose the laws that govern them – cannot exist without the rights to free speech, free press, free worship, and peaceable assembly.[5] A government that rules by the unrestrained will of the majority and does not respect those liberties is not free, even if it holds elections, but is only a waypoint on the road to servitude.[6] For under such government the minority, be it forty-nine percent or one-hundred-and-fifty-nine million citizens, is ever in danger of losing their inalienable rights to life, liberty, and the pursuit of happiness, because they, at sword-point, are neither permitted to object nor to organize in opposition to such affronts against their freedom. And once that minority loses their inalienable rights, the rights of the majority are soon lost too: because after the old majority has stripped the former minority of political rights and reduced them to servitude, a new majority eventually forms out of those who remain; and that new majority then strips forty-nine percent of the old majority of their rights and reduces them, too, to servitude. This process continues until no citizen holds power but one – the tyrant – at which point elections are done away with altogether or continued merely as a farce. So then does the Republic perish from the earth.

The corrosion of republics in this way has recurred throughout mankind's history. In the dying days of the Roman Republic, the populists led by Marius violently assailed the elitists, who returned under Sulla to trample the populists; then came Caesar and Pompey, then Antony and Augustus, until Rome was no longer a republic but a violent despotism suffering under the insane caprices of Nero and Caligula. The history of Germany in the 1930s, as it degenerated into the brutality of Nazism, also attests to illiberal democracy's inevitable result. There, those who manipulated the majority came first for Socialists, then for Jews, and then in stages brought repression, war, defeat, and ruin upon every citizen.[7] In our own age, we witnessed Venezuela's republic crumble. Chávez, elected by the people, broke the barriers that constrained him and violated the liberty of the minority which voted against him; now his successor watches with impunity as all the people starve. All of those nations were republics when they began their path to ruin; and no republic, if it fails to vigilantly guard its freedoms, is immune from their fate.

Be it known, then, the majority can have no political consciousness other than the words of a demagogue if ideas cannot be freely exchanged; all other rights, and all checks and balances in government, have no use if citizens' grievances cannot openly be aired; there will be grievous loss of life if peaceable assemblies are violently suppressed; there can be no liberty if contrary words are silenced; and no citizen may pursue happiness who is denied the free exercise of his or her faith. Government without these freedoms ceases to be a government of the people, by the people, for the people; it becomes first a government of the majority, by the majority, for the majority; and then it becomes inexorably a government of the tyrant, by the tyrant, for the tyrant. The Second Amendment preserves the sword that may, at last resort, be taken up by a free citizenry to defend itself from tyranny; but the First Amendment preserves the pen that allows the people to recognize tyranny when it appears, and to organize in struggle against it.[8]

We shall now, in the interest of preserving them, examine the present state of each of the First Amendment's freedoms: of speech, the press, peaceable assembly, and religion. Most have not yet been formally encroached upon by government, and those small intrusions that the federal and state governments have made on them have, for the time being, been justly rejected by our courts of law. Yet this happy state of affairs cannot be expected to continue if our public attitude becomes corrupted against these freedoms: the laws will eventually be undermined, the courts will grow silent, and despotism will creep forward.[9] It is therefore necessary for the citizens of our Republic to examine ourselves at regular intervals, so as to see if this corruption is creeping into our hearts; and if so, to reject it and instead stand firm in our convictions.

The First Amendment guarantees the right to free speech,

from which the right to free expression by other means may be derived. It does not, nor does any other article or amendment in the U.S. Constitution, guarantee a right not to be offended. The Declaration of Independence expresses an inalienable right only to pursue happiness; as the author of that venerable document might once have said, we must attain happiness ourselves.[10] Movements that seek to restrict free speech in order to protect sensitivities are contrary to the principles of free society. This is all the more so when they unfold in the nation's universities. Such places of learning, where the youth of future generations to whom we will someday entrust our Republic are forming their life-long convictions, ought to be open to the free exchange of ideas. Moreover, public universities, being as they are provided for by the States, are bound by law to be so.[11]

Freedom of expression extends also to history. Monuments and dedications, which are by their nature public in character, ought to be removed or altered by the majority vote of those who govern them,[12] not hastily purged at the demand of activists, however impassioned they may be. He who controls the past controls the future;[13] in a free society no individual or group ought to control the future, and so ought none to control the past by such means. If there is no consensus to discard the relics of past sins, build new statues to memorialize the aspirations of the present. Rather than censor the annals of history, write a new chapter through good works today.

We do not, by way of our defense of free speech, endorse hateful speech; such invective is unbecoming of the dignity of our Republic. Yet vile words do no injury to life or property. The notion of hate speech can never be so precisely defined that it will not, at some future time, be interpreted as to include speech that is merely considered offensive by one group or another. Such an ill-defined notion, were it to become a basis of law, would inevitably enable government to restrict any speech that it chooses; and government, by its nature, would then choose to restrict the speech which criticizes it. Thusly does liberty die. It is to the citizens of these United States, then, to rebut with our own dignified and respectful conduct those who spew forth hateful words. It is neither just nor wise to call upon the heavy hand of the state to do so.

Incitements and threats are another matter; both infringe upon the liberty of others.[14] No murderer ought to evade justice merely because his own hands did not hold the killing blade, if his words urged the one who held the blade to kill. Incitement to violence is thus rightly unlawful in these United States. Threats, even if they do not result in violence, are instruments of coercion that restrict liberty; they are likewise unlawful, and justly so.

Defamation, known too as slander or libel, can under certain circumstances impose social or monetary costs on people and firms; it is therefore just and proportionate that, in our Republic, those offenses are tried in a civil court, wherein those costs may be restituted to the plaintiff. Yet it is also to our Union's lasting credit that its standards of evidence for such complaints are more stringent than elsewhere in the world: the accused must have deliberately or recklessly spread a falsehood, rather than merely made an error or spoken the truth to one who wished to hide it.[15] In doubt, it is best to err on the side of liberty; exceptions to free speech are thus narrowly limited, and ought to remain so.

Yet there ought also to be a higher moral standard for public officials: that they ought not to disparage the exercise by others of those founding freedoms. For high officials hold the levers of government; their words signal the will of the state, and thereby cause the state's machinery to press upon those who do not possess such might. Thus do we turn to the next three freedoms.

The press, even at its best, will be flawed, and it may well be said that the press today is far from its best; but its freedom must nevertheless be sacrosanct.[16] Popular disdain for modern news practices does not override the First Amendment, and thus government may not lawfully take it upon itself to reform the failings of journalism. Yet today press freedom is ridiculed from the highest levels of authority. Such assaults are unacceptable in a republic: the use of political pressure on newspapers and other media outlets that criticize the policies or personalities of government is but a prelude to the use of violent force to silence opponents. If the people of these United States stand by and allow the free press to be shackled on account of its fleeting unpopularity, then there shall be no one to sound the alarm when the freedoms of the people are menaced in turn.[17] Citizens of this country are under no obligation to love the press; we may criticize it when it fails to uphold its standards; but we are nonetheless duty-bound by the principles underpinning our Republic to protect it from government coercion.

The exercise of the right to peaceable assembly, known as peaceful protest, has likewise fallen into contempt. Some officials, at the apex of our government, have in recent years reveled in the violent treatment of peaceable protestors. This, too, is unacceptable in a republic. Certain protests may be petty or foolish; but that they are petty or foolish has no bearing on the right of protestors to assemble. Other protests may call for policies that are harmful to the well-being of the Union, or even repugnant to the fundamental rights expressed in the First Amendment; but that they call for such harmful actions does not abrogate their right to gather together in peace.

There is but one distinction that matters: that protests are peaceable, or else are violent or threaten imminent violence. We hold, therefore, that mobs, which wantonly ruin life or property, are not peaceable protests, but riots; that 'armed protests,' if done to intimidate lawful authorities or seize public property, are not peaceable protests, but rebellions; and that the dispersal of either by government forces, through use of proportionate means, is justified by the Constitution, which refers often to the necessity of suppressing insurrection, rebellion, and lawless violence.[18]

The First Amendment guarantee of religious freedom contains two parts: it prohibits the establishment of a state religion – "Congress shall make no law respecting an establishment of religion…" – and it gives the citizen freedom to exercise his or her own faith – "…or prohibiting the free exercise thereof." The distinction between these parts appears clear, but often today they are invoked at cross-purposes; that is, the free exercise of religion is prohibited in the name of preventing religion's establishment.

The line ought justly to be drawn at the point of compulsion.[19] No citizen should be compelled in any matter of faith, unless that compulsion is to protect the constitutional rights of another citizen.[20] No Catholic organization therefore ought to be compelled to pay for insurance providing contraception, since such compulsion interferes with the free exercise of its faith;[21] but similarly, no insurance provider ought to be compelled by the government, for religious reasons, not to offer to the general public coverage providing contraception, for such compulsion would amount to an establishment of religion. Similarly, the First Amendment prevents religious rules, such as the Islamic sharia, from carrying the force of law. But were Congress to pass a law prohibiting the wear of the Islamic headscarf, such an act would prohibit the free exercise of our Muslim citizens' faith and thereby also violate the First Amendment. These and similar acts have been discussed or enacted in recent years, and will only continue; when they tend toward compulsion in affairs of faith, we as citizens must steadfastly oppose them.

It is not only the First Amendment that guards the essential rights of citizens in these United States. The Second and Third Amendments shield citizens from martial oppression; the Fourth through the Eighth Amendments ensure that tyrannical rule may not be imposed under the pretense of false justice; and the Thirteenth, Fourteenth, Fifteenth, and Nineteenth Amendments make clear beyond any shadow of doubt that citizenship in this Republic, and all the rights attendant upon it, stands independent of any criteria of race or sex.[22] As it is the duty of all citizens to uphold the entire Constitution of the United States, so must they guard vigilantly against infringement of all those parts of it. Yet the First Amendment is undoubtedly the foundation upon which those other freedoms have been upheld or gained; for without its guarantees of expression and assembly, citizens could never mobilize to demand their rights.

In the remaining essays in this series, we shall put forth particular proposals for action relating to the topic at hand. Yet we cannot propose legislation to protect these First

Amendment rights, because they are inscribed already in the Supreme Law of the Land. We can only maintain a constant vigilance and staunchly resist encroachments upon this first of laws and principles, regardless of whether those assaults are against the letter of the law or its spirit, and regardless of whether they are loud and aggressive or silent and furtive. We can demand that our legislators keep the First Amendment's freedoms foremost in their minds as they craft our laws; that our President enforce the laws faithfully and in a way that respects the aforementioned liberties; that the President nominate Justices and other officers of government who shall also uphold those freedoms; and that the Senate approve or reject those officers by weighing firstly whether or not they will guarantee the Constitution's promises of liberty. Lastly, we as citizens can and ought to vigorously defend these First Amendment freedoms in public debate, whether federal, state, or local; in the courts of law when serving as advocates, witnesses, or jurors; and in our interactions with fellow citizens, by whose vote legislators and the President are brought forth and recalled.

No. 2 – On Federalism

That a federal structure of government best preserves liberty in a large republic – That the United States today need decentralized and limited government – That the federal government ought to be vigorous in the exercise of its enumerated powers – That federalism encourages compromise and can alleviate the tyranny of the majority – That the multitude of States allows policy to be proven with minimal costs – That the partial sovereignty of the several States allows laws to match local values and conditions – That decentralization can give more political power to the individual citizen – That federalism checks tyrants and curbs excesses – That decentralization reduces bureaucracy – That a federal republic is more formidable in war and peace than a centralized one – That the enumerated powers granted to the federal government ought to be interpreted with restraint – That the several States ought to decentralize some power to their local governments

> "The powers not delegated to the United States by the Constitution, nor prohibited by it to the States, are reserved to the States respectively, or to the people." —**Tenth Amendment to the U.S. Constitution, ratified December 15th, 1791.**

NO. 2 – ON FEDERALISM

In our previous essay, we explained how the rights provided for in the First Amendment to the U.S. Constitution are fundamental to free government, and called for their staunch defense against the encroachment of 'illiberal democracy,' which is not free. Now we shall argue that the best structure for sustaining free government in a large republic, such as these United States, is a federal one; that the United States was founded as a Union of partly-sovereign States; that nine decades of relentless centralization have strained that Union; and that to preserve our Republic, what is now necessary is limited, decentralized, but also vigorous government at all levels.

We must first dwell momentarily on language, not only because doing so shall make this essay clearer, but because language shapes our perceptions. Today, the word "federal" and all its forms is often confused with the word "central," but ought not to be; a federal political system is a union of partly sovereign states, whereas a centralized political system vests all sovereignty in the central government. Perhaps consequently, the full name of the United States of America is now often truncated: the "United States" are dropped, and we are left only with "America." Similarly, "Union" has been all but lost from common use; it has been replaced by "Nation."

These semantics are significant, because the present usage misleads our perception of the great Union that we the people possess. The United States of America is a country conceived not as a uniform entity but as a federal Union of States, each subordinate to the whole but retaining certain sovereign powers. Among those are the authority of each State to raise its own revenue, to maintain its own militia, and to make its own laws, so far as those laws do not assume powers forbidden to the States by the U.S. Constitution or enumerated by the same for the federal head. The vast majority of day-to-day governing is thus meant to be done by the several States, which are closer to the people and therefore more responsive to their wants and needs. Even the most ardent of the classical Federalist advocates of strong union saw this division of power as the best solution to the challenge of governing a vast, continental Republic while also preserving liberty; so did the philosophers who inspired them.[23]

Yet, as the old idea of "Union" was replaced with the singular "Nation," the federal government encroached far upon the intended powers of the States. Departing from the balance carefully struck by Theodore Roosevelt and his fellow reformers at the turn of the 20th century, the administration of Franklin Roosevelt, in response to grave national crises, greatly expanded the federal government's scope. To overcome a World War and a Great Depression, he charged it with new duties in areas of governance, such as the provision of welfare and pensions, that had been left previously to the several States.[24] And even as memories of those trying times faded, Lyndon Johnson and subsequent presidents of both parties continued relentlessly to centralize power, such that the people now look to the administration in Washington, D.C., to provide for all of their wants and to redress all of their grievances. This state of affairs has polarized society and paralyzed government. It is our sincere desire to restore the Union to its proper balance.

Our stance may, at first glance, be viewed by some as a contradiction: the old Federalists, they might claim, pressed for a strong federal government to guard against encroachments by the States. Our response is that times have changed, but the desired end has not. Federalism is not centralism. In its early days, the Republic needed a more expansive and vigorous federal head in order to function properly as the federal Union that those Founders envisioned. Today, that very same end requires that the federal government exercise considerable restraint. Nor do limitation and restraint need translate into weakness, nor should they. Rather, the federal government ought to be energetic and supreme in exercising those powers that are clearly enumerated to it by the Constitution; and by focusing on those few prerogatives, rather than perpetuating its current diffuse and grasping sprawl, the federal government shall, in practice, be rendered more potent.[25]

We ought first to answer why a federal system is necessary for the preservation of liberty in these United States. It is to ensure that the leaders of a large republic, such as ours, govern in the interests of the people; that the rights and interests of any part of the people are not injured by the majority; and that control over the country cannot pass into the hands of a tyrant.

The material advantages of a large republic are readily apparent: a large country has more might to repel foreign aggressors, and more resources to devote to peacetime progress, than does a small country. Yet in a large republic, those who govern at the national level become distant from the governed. This is not necessarily due to arrogance or neglect on the part of those leaders, but simply a result of numbers: it is impossible for any one of them to become intimately familiar with the particular concerns of three-hundred-and-thirty million of their countrymen.[26] It is easier, relatively, for the governor and legislators of a small republic – in our case, the States – to know and understand the needs of their people;

and it is easier by far for a mayor or city councilperson to comprehend the needs of theirs. Thus, the more power is vested in governments that sit closer to the people, the more shall governance accord with the interests of the people.

Furthermore, that the passage of laws in a republic is done by the will of the majority is a just and acknowledged fact, for there exists no better way to obtain the consent of the governed. In every majority decision reached, however, there is a minority that has dissented from it, and that dissenting minority must nonetheless obey the law that is passed in such manner against its will, for the vote of the majority renders the law legitimate. Logically, there is some small loss of individual liberty therein on the part of the dissenters, as they are obligated to live with laws that they themselves did not assent to. This small cost to liberty is unavoidable in any system of government, and is far less egregious in democracy than under any other type of rule; but in a well-ordered federal republic it may be mitigated even further.

The smaller the dissenting minority in any political decision – in other words, the closer a vote comes to unanimity – the more closely the laws reflect the will of the entire people, and thus incur less loss to individual liberty. Unanimity, though rarely achieved, may be approached by means of compromise. Compromise in a large republic, possessed of a vast and diverse territory and population, is in the best of times a difficult feat. When, as now, the sheer number of citizens, in the hundreds of millions, reduces nearly all people to anonymity in the eyes of their fellow countrymen, compromise becomes harder still. It is in human nature to be reluctant to harm one's close acquaintances, yet it is easy, without thinking, to reject out of hand the needs of strangers. At the local and state levels of government, kinship, neighborliness, or at least a basic familiarity acquired by living in close proximity tend to give one's fellow citizens a human face; it follows that political decisions, if made in neighborhoods, towns, counties, cities, and states, ought to be likelier to result in compromise than if those decisions were made at the federal level.

In addition, a large republic has distinct regions, each of which by nature requires certain necessities for its inhabitants' well-being. Citizens living within a particular region thus usually hold at least some common interests, which derive from the common needs of life in that area. Compromise and a semblance of unanimity are thus likelier to result from decisions made within regions than across them.[27] And, in the last case, a dissenting minority that results from a regional decision will nonetheless, in most instances, have had its concerns heard and considered more by the regional government, which is close, than by the national government, which is distant.

Nonetheless, it is true, sometimes disputes arise in towns and cities that are as vicious and unyielding as those that arise in nations; sometimes the hatreds such disputes produce can lead to violence and oppression as severe at the local level as at the national. Yet even in these worst of instances, when neighbor sets upon neighbor, a well-functioning federal system can mitigate the harm. When a city or state, facing a controversial decision, is consumed by hostile passions that flow from it, the federal head may intervene to ensure the rights of citizens.[28] A central system offers no such succor: as few decisions are left to towns and regions, the bitterest controversies necessarily become national; few things but civil war or foreign intervention may resolve them.

Moreover, federalism is the last and strongest check against the establishment of tyranny. All governments, even those elected by the people, are corruptible, because all governments are the work of mankind, and mankind is corruptible. For that reason, our Republic's Founders instituted a separation of powers between the executive, legislative, and judicial branches of the federal government, and devised checks and balances among them. Rather than trust only in mankind's virtue, they contrived that no man or woman could acquire unchallenged power over the Union. They did so skillfully. A would-be tyrant in these United States faces a daunting task: he, or she, must first deceive a majority of the people to be elected to high office; he must then dominate the Congress, then suborn the courts, and then bend to his will all fifty of the States.[29]

That final task, of subjugating the States, is for the tyrant the most difficult of all. The Congress and the courts wield the power of the law; but when a chief executive holds the law in contempt, the legislative and judicial branches do not themselves have the means to prevent him from enacting his despotic designs. Yet the state governments, by withholding their cooperation, may render his unlawful demands impotent. The several States, for instance, each hold authority over the police forces, without which no act of oppression can effectively be carried out. Moreover, States may, through appeals in the courts, lend their resources to the re-establishment of the law. That they shall indeed act in such a way is likely, for, in federal republics such as ours, history has shown that some states are always governed by the opposition party; those states, at least, would be willing to resist tyranny in a time of need.[30]

It can thus be said that, in a well-functioning federal republic, the states comprise the last separation of power, after the division of the federal executive, legislature, and judiciary.[31] But if that federal system should fail – if, by the creeping encroachment of central authority over the powers reserved to the several States, those States are rendered fully dependent on whomever controls the government of the Union – then the tyrant's hardest work will have already been done for him, and establishing his dominion over every part of the Republic shall be made easy.

Thus does a federal structure of government, in conjunction with the rights enshrined within the First Amendment and elsewhere in the Constitution that are guaranteed to all citizens by the federal government, soften the tyranny of the majority and thereby preserve liberty.

We shall now endeavor to describe some of the practical benefits of true federalism – of reserving sufficient powers to the States – to the Union as a whole, though we shall not attempt to restate all of the arguments made in 1787 by the classical Federalists and their rivals. Rather, we shall focus on what is today most overlooked: that the diversity of state laws and governing systems in these United States, fifty at present, is far more a strength than it is a hindrance.

First, the federal structure of the United States provides a multitude of testing grounds for new policies, the effects of which are unknown until somewhere put into practice. Should some previously untested policy fail in one State, the effects of its failure will be limited: they will be largely confined to that State, rather than unleashed upon the Union as a whole. The other States, observing that failure, might then not be tempted to attempt the same policy, thus sparing their residents from its disastrous effects. Conversely, if a new policy should succeed brilliantly in one State, the others might then be inspired to mimic it, thus sharing its benefits as effectively as if it had been imposed all at once by the federal head, but without the danger of the latter method.

Second, the partial sovereignty of the several States allows for legislation to be adapted to local conditions. When Congress passes a law for the whole Republic, it is nearly unavoidable that certain provisions of it shall neglect the regional interests of some parts of the Union. Such omissions may occur even if the intention of the federal legislators is benevolent, because it is nearly impossible to make even a small adjustment to a large and complex republic without disrupting some part of it. If, instead, the governments of the parts – the States – decide the matter with separate legislation, they are less likely to neglect the unique interests of their residents. That is, a law that brings benefit to the citizens of New Jersey might bring ruin if adopted in Oklahoma; thus, unless it is both necessary and constitutional that the law be imposed upon the entire Union, it is far better that one law be adopted in New Jersey and that a different law be adopted in Oklahoma, so that each State may therefore prosper in its own manner.

Third, a decentralized approach to social issues ought to alleviate the "culture wars" that have so damagingly polarized our country. Such controversies, as they are closely tied to the personal convictions of citizens, inflame the passions of many; for that reason, they do not lend themselves easily to compromise. The fear that the federal government might decide those affairs in one party's favor has produced only the result of making each national election into a vicious struggle for domination, in which the loser sees no recourse. Thus do factional divisions harden.

Take, by way of example, two of the bitterest disputes in our Republic today: those over regulation of firearms and abortions. The many whose passions are ignited by those matters often suspect that their fellow citizens are plotting to restrict their personal liberties, and so they view their own countrymen as enemies. We posit that a majority of Texans may breathe easier if they need not fear imposition of New York's gun-control laws in their own State, whereas a majority of New Yorkers may be more at ease if they do not fear that Texans are scheming to impose their laws regulating abortion upon New York. Such limitation of federal authority over those affairs, although the rhetoric of both major parties makes it appear outlandish, is in fact the status quo. The Constitution, in the first instance, and Supreme Court precedent, in the second, allow for a similar interpretation on arms and abortion: that States may regulate each, but prohibit neither.[32]

Were the national parties to cease their efforts to legislate or adjudicate such social affairs at the federal level, it may be argued, those controversies would nonetheless burn with the same intensity in the several States. That is true, but some of their ill-effects shall be mitigated. Those dissenters who lose the majority vote within each individual State may, as citizens of the United States, move to and become resident in another State with laws more to their preference. If they prefer instead to remain and press for change, they shall at least do so amongst their neighbors, rather than strangers with whom empathy is less easily felt. In either instance, they need not have enmity towards people of another State who do not share their cultural preferences. Residents of Maryland and of Wyoming can both be proud Americans and consider the other also to be so; though each lives in a different manner, each may be trusted not to interfere in the manner of the other. When the federal government takes social affairs into its own hands, such harmony cannot exist. Better, then, to regulate them in state legislatures, to whom the Constitution reserves such power, so that when change comes, the people know and feel that they themselves decided it.

That is not to say that there should not be some common national aspects of culture, but they should be limited to things directly necessary to the preservation of the Union, such as love of liberty and respect for the law. We do say that the government is not, nor ought to be, the prime determiner of culture. Rather, it ought to allow society's healthy and natural development by refraining from regulating cultural matters that have little bearing on high functions of state.

Fourth, the proper reservation of powers to state and local governments enables ordinary citizens to be more engaged in, and able to influence, their own governance. Our Republic works on the principle of one person, one vote. Yet one individual vote out of the two hundred million that comprise the eligible population of the United States will seem to most citizens like a mere raindrop in the ocean. That perception leads the individual to despair of his or her right to have a say in government; that despair tempts many, as we see today, to turn away from enlightened government to the false prophets of illiberal democracy. Yet it is easier for citizens to achieve a political goal in their State; it is even easier in their county; and it is easier still in their town or neighborhood. The more governance is left to those smaller electorates, the more shall individual citizens see their own hand in it, and be content to be governed by republican means.

Fifth, even in times when the Republic is not threatened by a tyrant, the States may act as a check on the excesses of the federal executive when Congress does not, thereby encouraging prudence and moderation in federal policies. For instance, state governments have the standing to challenge a policy in the federal courts, on the question of that policy's adherence to the U.S. Constitution; vigorous States may make constructive use of this ability.

Sixth, decentralized decision-making in government reduces the need for a multiplicity of rules and regulations, thus reducing the paralyzing burden of bureaucracy currently imposed upon our governments and enterprises. Rules are instituted in the place of discretion; when the lower levels of government may exercise greater discretion, fewer rules are needed from the higher levels. We shall discuss this advantage more extensively in another essay.

Seventh, a union composed of several diverse parts is more formidable in war and peace than a centralized nation of similar size, provided that its federal head can mobilize the resources of the union in times of crisis. Should some calamity throw its federal head into disorder, it is able to carry on: states and cities, accustomed already to governing themselves, shall continue to act in the absence of instructions from the center. In the peacetime endeavors of industry and innovation, an entrepreneur may choose, from a variety of options, the state or city whose unique laws are most suitable for his or her idea to flourish. The flexibility displayed in the latter case builds national strength; the resilience illustrated in the former instance preserves it.

We have thus far discussed why the preservation of a federal structure of government is desirable and why its erosion in the past century is damaging to our Union; what remains is to say how the federal system has been eroded and how might it be restored. We must first note that the steady expansion of central power since the mid-20th century is not strictly unconstitutional: many Presidents and leaders of both parties, often with noble intentions, made use of open-ended clauses of the Constitution to put forth their agenda in Congress and defend it before the courts. That practice continues today, contrary to the spirit of the founding document but not its letter.

The 'Necessary and Proper' clause in Article 1, Section 8, the article of the Constitution that enumerates the powers of the federal Congress, was denounced by Anti-Federalists during the ratification debate as a blank check for federal power; but that clause does no more than give Congress the means to legislate in order to achieve the ends that the Constitution already granted it.[33] The true loop-holes are in the vague description of one enumerated power, "to provide for the general Welfare of the United States," and the broad interpretation of another, "to regulate Commerce among the several States." Almost any law may be characterized as providing for the general welfare, and the great proportion of laws which in some way affect the national economy may be portrayed as regulation of interstate commerce. Thus are the doors open to an unlimited expansion of federal control over matters reserved to the States, or to the people.

It might be argued, then, that the Constitution ought to be amended so as to withdraw those two powers from Congress.

Yet to do so would be rash and foolish, because situations exist in which it is both entirely appropriate and within the spirit of the Constitution for Congress to legislate on those pretexts. Preventing Congress from regulating interstate commerce would stunt the economy both of the Union and of the several States: witness the tangle of conflicting state regulations across the sea in India, whose government today fights to overcome that discord and unleash the country's vast potential. There are also some issues that require a national response – that is, they cannot be effectively addressed by the States alone – but that cannot be characterized under any other enumerated power but for the general welfare of the United States. There also ought to be allowances for instances in which a well-crafted federal law can reduce the volume of bureaucracy formed by successive layers of local and state government.[34]

The necessary and proper response to the creep of central power in these United States, therefore, is not to re-write the constitutional rules of government, which at any rate are always open to interpretation and wrangling, but instead to elect officials, at all levels of government, who exercise discretion and restraint in keeping with the spirit of the Constitution, rather than its letter alone; who trust in a federal system, in which the component parts enjoy and may exercise some portion of sovereignty; who take a narrower view on the powers enumerated to the federal government, and a more expansive view on the powers reserved to the States, or to the people; who refrain from supporting bills proposed under the powers of interstate commerce or general welfare, unless those bills be truly necessary to the Union's well-being and cannot effectively be addressed by local or state laws alone; and who are nonetheless committed to the full and vigorous exercise of federal authority under powers clearly enumerated to the federal government in letter and in spirit, such as providing for the national defense and managing the national debt.

Some may object that decentralization leads not always to greater compromise but, where certain prejudices exist, to the subjugation of a minority by the local majority. We do not deny that this phenomenon has occurred, in grievous form, at intervals throughout the history of our Republic; our bloodiest war was instigated by the leaders of a rebellion which sought to preserve the evil of slavery behind a thin veneer of "states' rights." That Civil War ended, however, with a series of Amendments to the Constitution of the United States that removed all doubt from the founding principle that all Americans are equal before the law. It remains the duty of the federal government to uphold those Amendments, just as it is that government's duty to uphold the entire Constitution; no federalist creed may justly sanction the denial of constitutional rights.[35]

We shall also note here a most crucial exception to our general theory, which is that the federal government must be able to concentrate power in times of grave crisis, so as to mobilize the resources of the entire Republic to overcome the danger. It is no coincidence that previous broad expansions of federal power occurred during the Civil War, the World Wars, and the Great Depression. Our objection is not that Lincoln and F.D.R. took those actions in the midst of crisis, but that, principally in the latter case, their successors failed to restore the federal balance once those crises had receded, and instead clung to centralization in hope of exercising similar power as their wartime predecessors. In so doing, they drained the long-term strength of our Union.[36]

Finally, the States ought not to demand decentralization from the federal government if they are not willing in turn to offer some decentralization to their own cities and counties; and those cities and counties ought not to demand that their state governments cede powers to them if they are not willing to cede powers to their neighborhoods or municipalities, and so on down to the individual citizen. Thus, we call for the election of legislators and officials who are willing to amend and interpret state constitutions and city charters to provide for a more decentralized, federal character; who are, ultimately, willing to trust the citizen with his or her own affairs, recognizing that the people's ability to govern themselves increases at each level of government that is closer to them, their immediate surroundings, and their day-to-day lives.

Federalism carries risks: some States, cities, towns, or neighborhoods will fail, and thus a wise government has emergency provisions in place, such as laws governing bankruptcy. But it also promotes responsibility and rewards success; like a free market, it relinquishes some central control in exchange for greater dynamism and enterprise. Moreover, it is the structure of government most conducive to the preservation of liberty across a vast population and territory such as that of these United States. It therefore ought to be jealously guarded and perpetuated.

No. 3 – On Representative Government

That democracy ought to be more direct the nearer that government is to the people – That it ought to be more by representation the farther that government is from the people – That States and local entities ought to have some representation as a body politic in higher levels of government – That the practice of legislation by referendum ought to be curtailed – That outside financing ought to be restricted in state and local elections – That a well-functioning federal system weakens special interests – That electoral districts ought to be drawn in accordance with community boundaries – That the 17th Amendment ought to be refined – That citizens ought to trust in their representatives – That representatives ought to lead

> "A Republic, by which I mean a Government in which the scheme of representation takes place, opens a different prospect, and promises the cure for which we are seeking. Let us examine the points in which it varies from pure Democracy, and we shall comprehend both the nature of the cure, and the efficacy which it must derive from the Union."
> **—James Madison, *Federalist No. 10*, November 22nd, 1787.**

NO. 3 – ON REPRESENTATIVE GOVERNMENT

In our previous essay, we argued that the United States ought to restore its federal character by returning to the several States their due part of sovereignty. This task cannot be done without also reinforcing the system of representation that supports such a wide and diverse Union. The framers of this country's Constitution intended that it be governed as a republic; not, in most instances, by the people directly, but through the representatives of each State or district, who are accountable to the people through periodic elections. They did so because history had taught them, through examples ancient and modern, that if a country so vast as these United States of America were to be governed as a direct democracy, it would, through the deceptions of ambitious swindlers, descend first into a tyranny of the majority and from there inevitably into a tyranny of one.[37] Indeed today, when technology has made it possible for polls to be taken at a moment's notice, and when cable news and the internet have made every citizen consider him- or herself an able judge of national questions, direct democracy has returned to our Republic in grotesque form.[38-39] It is no coincidence that with it have returned demagogues and would-be tyrants, who embrace illiberal democracy to enrich themselves and feed their lust for power. To counter this destructive drift, our Republic must adopt reforms which shall restore to its elected representatives the responsibility and will to lead, and which shall likewise restore to the people the confidence in their representatives that makes republican government possible.

There are two principles that relate to the necessity and structure of representative government. The first involves the ability of the people directly to make wise decisions at the various levels of government. Some urbane citizens, arrogant and aloof, denounce the common man and woman as stupid or degenerate. That conclusion is wrong, and leads only towards the establishment of aristocracy and the loss of freedom for all. The proportion of men and women who are stupid or degenerate is small, and the common man is neither a fool nor depraved; he has in him basic human decency and is not deceived in things with which he is familiar.[40] Most people, both rich and poor, are, however, narrow-minded: our understanding and desires are limited by our personal experience, which cannot encompass everything. Most people tend also to be short-sighted, desiring that which offers us immediate advantage and neglecting that which would benefit us in the future. But those detriments are different from stupidity or degeneracy, and understanding them allows us to structure an effective scheme of representative government.[41]

Because most men and women understand very well those matters that surround them and affect their daily lives, democracy ought to be the most direct at the local level. This is doubly so because of the small number of citizens that makes up a community: it is easier to reach compromise and consensus with your neighbors, whose circumstances you know and understand, than it is with an anonymous multitude. Therefore, decisions reached by a majority in local votes are less likely to be unbearable to those who dissented. As the people themselves can thus be expected to make wiser and more accommodating decisions at the local level of government, municipal constitutions should allow a maximum of direct democratic participation.

At the state level, the matters at hand are often a step removed from daily life, and their consequences are less immediate; state governments thus require wider knowledge and greater foresight. We must therefore revisit the human shortcomings discussed above. Whereas there is no remedy for stupidity or depravity, an education can remedy narrow-mindedness and short-sightedness by informing its recipient of possibilities outside his or her personal experience.[42] A state is thus governed better when the people choose learned citizens from amongst themselves to govern it, then hold those legislators and officers accountable through periodic elections. It follows that federal lawmaking and administration, which demand thorough understanding of the arts and sciences of economics, diplomacy, and war, ought to be done primarily by the most experienced and knowledgeable of citizens, so long as they win the people's confidence through election.[43] As such, while direct democracy is appropriate at the local level, governance ought to be done increasingly by representation at the state and federal levels to diminish the probability of unwise choices caused by the most natural, widespread, and correctable of human limitations.

We do not say, however, that education makes a particular citizen superior to his fellow countrymen, for not every citizen needs an extensive education to make an honorable living. Furthermore, human vices such as greed or jealousy cannot be corrected by education, and thus ought to be considered a constant, affecting in equal proportions both the common man and the highest magistrates. And we shall also note that an education can be self-obtained; it need not be accompanied by a lofty university degree, nor indeed any degree at all. Education is simply the broadening of understanding beyond personal experience through the acquisition of knowledge, and the citizen who possesses an education, however he or she achieved it, can render effective service in the administration of their State and the Republic, if held to account through elections. The history of our Republic attests to this truth: neither George Washington nor Harry Truman was college-educated, but each took the time to teach himself; each proved a capable President.

The second principle applying to representative government is that it is necessary for communities and States to be represented as political bodies in higher levels of government in order to govern themselves effectively and independently. The Constitution of the United States is federal in structure, in that its authority is drawn from both the several States and the whole of the people of the United States.[44] States are represented in the Senate, the people are represented in the House of Representatives, and through the Electoral College both the States and the people are represented in the election of Presidents.[45] That the interests of each State are represented in Congress is necessary to the well-being of the Union, because otherwise the federal government would be moved only by national majorities of citizens and thus driven to ignore the distinctions between States when crafting laws and policies. Such neglect would undermine the ability of the several States to govern themselves using the powers reserved to them by the Constitution. If the people wish to manage the affairs of their own State, thereby shielding themselves from the tyranny of the national majority, they must allow some of their representation at the federal level to flow through their State, rather than from them directly. The same principle applies to representation of counties and cities in state governments and of wards and neighborhoods in city governments.

We have established, then, that these United States are meant to be governed as a Republic, not a direct democracy; that the exercise of democracy ought to be the most direct at local levels of government and the most indirect at the federal level; that the several States, though their duly elected governments, ought themselves to be represented in some manner in the federal government; and that the same principle ought to apply to the representation of municipalities in state governments. From these conclusions follow several proposals.

First, the practice of legislating through referendum, abused of late by state governments, ought to be curtailed.[46] Using popular referendums to pass laws does not make government more enlightened, but merely confuses it. The practice undermines state legislatures, which under the constitutions of every State are the bodies empowered to propose, debate, and pass laws. If the legislature forfeits its legislative function to the people, then why does it exist in the first place?

It exists for the reason discussed above, that the people as a whole are focused on their daily lives and have little time or inclination to ponder the future of their State; therefore, they delegate legislative authority to individuals of their choosing, who may devote their full knowledge and attention to that task. Thus, on balance, laws passed by elected legislators at the state level will be wiser and more effective than laws passed directly by the people. Nor can it be pretended that state legislatures lack democratic legitimacy or proper accountability: a popular referendum is built into them, at set intervals, through the election of their members. When those representatives, through laziness or timidity, cede their lawmaking function back to the people, they discard the system of governing that the people themselves have established for their own benefit. This to us smells of negligence.

That is not to say that there are never extraordinary situations in which a question of great import ought rightly to be put before the people; but those situations ought to be extraordinary, not routine. When such matters arise, they might often be better addressed by use of conventions, rather than referendums. In that method, the broad question is presented to the people, and they elect a special convention of delegates, independent of the legislature, to debate the matter and decide upon a resolution. Such a method, as was used to ratify the Constitution of the United States, allows the people to weigh in upon the issue at hand – as the citizens whom they would choose as their convention delegates would need, in order to be elected, to make their mind on the particular question known – while avoiding the shortfall of direct democracy at higher levels of government, namely that the people may be called upon to decide the details of an issue with which they are not familiar.[47]

Second, the use of funds from outside of a State ought to be restricted in the elections of that State, and the same principle should apply also to local elections. That money is useful and influential in an election campaign is well known to all of us citizens of the United States in the present era; so with what justice should a candidate for office in Montana gain an advantage through funds drawn from Virginia? This practice infringes upon the sovereignty of the State and on the right of the people in that State to determine their own affairs; it has the effect of subordinating one State to another, or of unconstitutionally subordinating the State to the federal whole. The role of private finance in election contests generally is a broader question, open to reasonable debate; the use of outside funds to intervene in state and local elections is hardly defensible and ought to be curtailed.

A note is appropriate here on the subject of lobbying and special interests, which popular consensus holds, with some basis, to be both rampant and corrosive to representative government in our Republic.[48] A properly functioning federal system, however, works naturally against the ability of wealthy interests to unduly influence elected representatives. In one aspect, it disperses and dilutes the efforts of those who would influence with money the workings of government. When more decisions are reserved to state and local governments, special interests must, with the same amount of resources, attempt to target many more officials and representatives. Rather than win the ear of one hundred U.S. Senators, they must instead attempt to woo several hundred state senators; rather than whisper in the ear of one President, they must try to reach fifty governors. Thus, if corruption enters into one part of the Union, the others may remain sound.

Also, it is in the conduct of election campaigns that politicians become most susceptible to moneyed influence; this is because campaigns for high office have become excessively expensive on account of the need to reach millions of eligible voters. State and local campaigns need to reach fewer citizens; they therefore require less money; and candidates are more able to raise a smaller sum from ordinary citizens, and so rely less on large donations from interested parties. Moreover, local representatives are closer to the people; they are thus more easily scrutinized by the citizens they represent, and so corruption may be more easily discovered and exposed.

Third, electoral districts for the U.S. House of Representatives ought to be drawn contiguously and in accordance with existing administrative lines. This is to say that, as far as possible, county and city boundaries ought to be used as the boundaries for electoral districts, and adjacent counties and cities ought to be grouped together when proportionality in population requires them to be combined into districts. Partisan gerrymandering is as old as our Republic, yet modern technology has enabled it to become obscene. The distortions it causes, by relegating all meaningful electoral competition to party primaries, are well known and discussed. We base our argument on a federalist foundation: the fragmentation of electoral districts to suit partisan ends denies actual communities any true representation in their highest level of government. Just as it benefits the Republic that the States are represented in the Senate, so is it healthy that counties and cities find some measure of representation in the House. Members of Congress who are charged through their election with acting on behalf of a real community, which has distinct interests based upon common needs of life and not upon ideology alone, shall be imbued with a feeling of duty to that community, rather than solely to their national party.

Finally, the 17th Amendment to the United States Constitution ought to be refined. That amendment, which transferred election of Senators from the state legislatures to the people directly, has undermined the constitutional purpose of the Senate to represent the several States. The federal system, as discussed above, was designed deliberately to draw legitimacy from both the people and the States; hence why all States are represented equally in the Senate, but are represented proportionally by population in the House. That the election of Senators by state governments was useful for the representation of state interests was hardly debated before the Constitution's ratification: our Founders were confident that the legislatures of each State would be more focused upon the long-term needs of the State and the intricacies of the issues facing it, than would the general citizenry.[49]

The Founders' method of electing Senators also served the second purpose of the Senate: to enable consistency and far-sightedness in its functions by insulating it from the ever-changing currents of public opinion.[50] But the 17th Amendment, which was intended to serve this aim by shielding Senators from the self-interest of state politicians, has in recent years instead placed their nomination into the unsteady hands of party primaries, which often present the people with only extremists to choose from. Nor can the length of a Senator's term alone permit him or her to chart a steady course if, every few years at the end of it, he or she is reduced to thoughtless and inconsistent pandering to obtain a nomination for re-election.[51] In this way, the 17th Amendment has reduced the Senate to a mere copy of the House of Representatives, which was established by the Founders to represent the people directly, with all of their momentary passions.[52]

Yet to repeal the 17th Amendment would be to move too far in correction of the problem that exists. The argument for that amendment's adoption had some sound logic to it. The election of a Senator, who serves for six years and may not be recalled,[53] is a significant commitment; as the Senator will continue to represent the State even if the composition of the state government changes during that term, it is appropriate that he or she receives some mandate from the people.

We thus propose that the 17th Amendment be modified to provide for the nomination of candidates for the U.S. Senate by vote of party caucuses within each state legislature, and for the Senator to be elected from among those candidates by the people of that State. For instance, all the Democratic state legislators shall convene to choose the Democratic nominee; Republican legislators shall likewise nominate the Republican candidate; and in the same manner shall other parties represented in the state legislature select their candidates;[54] those candidates shall then go to the people for a general election. This method returns to the state governments some hand in the election of Senators, thereby reinvigorating the federal system, while leaving to the people the final say, so to ensure that the Senator's mandate shall extend through his or her full term.

The success of these proposals, and of a republic generally, requires that the people place some trust in their elected representatives, and that they expect them to think, decide, and lead, rather than merely follow the polls.[55] It is common to hear complaints today that representatives are corruptly beholden to some special interest, but this charge can be thrown back to the citizen. Representatives are, in the final reckoning, beholden only to the people: perhaps the sole salutary effect of the election of 2016 is that it demonstrated vividly to many who had grown cynical that their vote is counted; that it is not, in fact, 'rigged.' If, citizen, you desire honest government, then vote for honest men and women to be your representatives; and if you voted for one who seemed honest, but became corrupt, then throw him out at the next election and replace him with one better. Use your vote, too, to make the prestige of office a reward for distinguished service to town, State, or Union; make election the culmination of duty, not a step in a career that puts talk above service, nor a birthright, nor a final grab in a life of self-enrichment. We have had enough of that. Let us preserve our Republic; be thankful that we choose our representatives; hold them accountable at elections; and expect them to govern, for that is what we have elected them to do.

No. 4 – On Bureaucracy

That Congress ought not to delegate legislative power to executive agencies – That excessive regulation infringes liberty and impedes federalism – That federal legislation ought to be concise, but local legislation may be nuanced – That sunset clauses ought to be added to laws which grant wide discretion to the executive – That Congress and the executive ought to discard outdated laws and regulations – That the size of the Cabinet ought to be reduced – That the States ought to be given discretion in how they attain federal standards – That the capacity of the judicial branch ought to be increased – That complex federal laws and regulation are necessary for some objects

> "It will be of little avail to the people that the laws are made by men of their own choice, if the laws be so voluminous that they cannot be read, or so incoherent that they cannot be understood; if they be repealed or revised before they are promulged, or undergo such incessant changes that no man who knows what the law is today can guess what it will be tomorrow." —**James Madison, *Federalist No. 62*, February 27th, 1788.**

NO. 4 – ON BUREAUCRACY

In our previous essay, we upheld the necessity of representative government in a large republic and examined the consequences that occur when elected representatives cede legislative authority back to the people. Here, we explore the consequences that occur when representatives instead abdicate that authority to an unelected bureaucracy. It is the unfortunate condition of our Republic today that its laws resemble those deplored by Mr. Madison; and by being in such a state they have upended the separation of powers that, after much toil and sacrifice against the consolidated power of the British Crown, was enshrined in the Constitution of the United States.

These United States have arrived at such a state of affairs because Congress has in past decades wantonly delegated power to regulatory agencies by means of poorly-crafted laws, such that the executive branch has now come to wield immense legislative authority. A President may, by issuing an executive order or announcing an emergency, effect sweeping changes in policy or transfer billions of dollars in public funds – powers that the Founders of our Republic bestowed on Congress.[56] Even in the absence of Presidential direction, bureaucratic agencies continuously promulge regulations that, though not called laws, are legally binding upon citizens. Laws meant for the people's well-being thus instead pull lawmaking farther from the people; they constrain state and local governments; and they multiply rules that suffocate enterprise and governance, thereby sapping our Union's vigor. It is our view that new laws ought to be designed so as to limit the federal bureaucracy; that bad laws and unnecessary regulation ought to be discarded; and that regulation which remains necessary, with some exceptions, ought to give wider discretion to the States.

Our argument is founded upon the principle of non-delegation, that the elected legislature has no right to give its lawmaking function to any other person or body. This principle derives from the fundamental premise on which our Republic is founded, that all legitimate government derives from the consent of the governed – that is, from the people. The people, being unable to exercise direct democracy over a vast country, vest legislative power in a representative body of their choosing.[57] In these United States, the people, having ratified the Constitution, bestowed this power on Congress. As Congress is the sole body in the federal government fully representative of the people, it may not cede its authority to make laws to any other institution, for laws created in such a way would not derive from the consent of the people and would thus be illegitimate.[58]

In recent decades, Congress has grown desirous of crafting exhaustive laws which would govern every matter that society may encounter. Yet it is beyond the ability of legislators to accomplish in detail the task they set for themselves: they have other legislation to attend to, and so cannot devote their full time to the comprehensive law they seek. To close the gap between ambition and reality, they include provisions which empower a regulatory agency to extrapolate the meaning of the law to particular instances, and thereupon to publish detailed rules that carry the law's force. The law's practical effect on citizens is manifested in such particulars, and so the law comes to be defined by those regulations created by executive agencies, which are not representative of the people. By venturing to leave no aspect of life unlegislated, Congress has thus fallen into the habit of delegating legislative power, depriving the people of consent.

It must also be noted that voluminous and incoherent laws cede authority not only from the people to the bureaucracy, but from the people to lawyers and to those wealthy enough to employ lawyers. If only those who have devoted years to the study of law can understand the laws, it will be only they and those who can most readily access their services who will benefit from the law itself; whereas ordinary citizens will be perplexed and thus left helpless before the executive, whose arbitrary interpretations of the law they do not know how to challenge.[59] This, we venture to proclaim, is very much the condition of our Republic today.

Furthermore, complex federal laws and a multitude of regulations impede the functioning of a federal republic by constraining the laws of the States. Each new federal law or regulation on a given matter restricts the ability of state legislatures to design their own laws affecting that matter, thereby restricting the partial sovereignty that the States under the Constitution are meant to enjoy. This principle applies also to the effect of state laws and regulation upon municipalities.

From these general principles three particular ones may be derived, which serve as a guide to responsible legislation. First, laws ought not to be made at all unless they are necessary and proper to the ends defined by the federal or state constitutions, and in all other instances it is best to leave decisions to individuals, organizations, and lower governments. This preference rests on the reasoning that the benefit of new laws to society must outweigh the cost of adding to the body of laws.[60] That cost is both monetary, in that fewer laws require fewer resources to be spent on enforcement, and political, in that the absence of a law governing a particular aspect of life allows individual citizens to enjoy personal choice, the maximization of which is one of the principal aims of enlightened government.

Second, laws ought to be simple and well-defined, so as to limit the regulator's scope for extrapolation. This preference addresses the non-delegation principle. If the laws that Congress passes are concise and clear, they shall require fewer regulations to supplement them, and those regulations which must be made can more easily be scrutinized to ensure that they are strictly pursuant to the law from which they arise, and do not exceed it. Moreover, the people themselves will be able to evaluate the laws passed in their name, and to weigh their findings in their choice of legislators, thus ensuring that their original authority to give assent is not removed from them.

Third, the preceding two principles apply proportionally less strictly at lower levels of government. This preference addresses the fact that sometimes, in order to maintain liberty, complex laws are indeed necessary, so as to accommodate the great variety of circumstances that affect the lives of citizens.[61] Yet such complexities are best crafted and enacted at the local level. Local laws often function more effectively than sweeping federal laws, as they are adapted to local circumstance, and better safeguard liberty, as the people have more direct input in their design. For this reason, the power of making ordinary criminal laws, which have the greatest effect on personal liberty, is reserved to the States.[62] It follows that federal laws, in most cases, are improved if they allow refinement at lower levels. There are certain exceptions, particularly for laws governing commerce that extends across state boundaries; we shall return to these later.

There are also practical reasons to curtail the federal bureaucracy. The complexity of laws yields a multiplicity of regulations pursuant to them; a multiplicity of regulations produces a multiplicity of agencies to promulge and enforce them; and a multiplicity of agencies produces a multiplicity of budgets to carry out their operations. This tangled web of rules paralyzes our government's capacity for action, while this multitude of costs adds to the burden of taxation and debt. Not only are time, money, and effort buried in this way, but the very impulse for action is stifled, and an inert mindset develops. This malaise first affects government, but if not checked spreads to private enterprise; if it is not reversed, society and the economy become stagnant, and then decline.[63] This effect was evident in France, where excessive labor laws paralyzed industry and suppressed employment; the French today are laboring to reform those rules. It ought not to be forgotten that the ideas of enlightened government and the free market developed hand in hand: each reinforces the other, and together they enable civilization to thrive.

Perhaps, some will say, though a huge mass of regulation may be an evil, it is nonetheless a necessary evil for administering a large country. Yet the experience of the British shows that a vast bureaucracy is as unnecessary as it is harmful: the British Empire, at its height, governed one-quarter of the world with fewer than fifty thousand civil servants.[64] They did it by limiting their central government and instead entrusting authority to the governments of their territories and dominions. These United States may rival that feat, in governing its own large territory and populace, by limiting its federal bureaucracy and entrusting authority to the several States; and it may do so more effectively than the British did, because the state governments, unlike those of Britain's former imperial territories, are accountable to their people. To do so, however, reform and restructuring must be had, for which we shall now offer some particular proposals.

First, the volume of federal laws and regulations ought to be reduced, and kept thereafter at the lowest level necessary to meet public needs. Certain steps may be taken immediately – some have already been initiated – to achieve this aim gradually and without harm to the public interest. Congress ought to include "sunset clauses" in laws that delegate regulatory power to the executive branch, thereby requiring that those laws, and regulations issued pursuant to them, be reviewed periodically by Congress itself; though the period between reviews ought to be long enough that firms and citizens affected by the law are not forced constantly to adjust to changes which may be made upon review. Additionally, a commission ought to be established to review antiquated laws and recommend them to Congress for repeal; and the executive branch ought continually to review and eliminate outdated regulations and uphold policies that require old regulations to be removed prior to the introduction of new ones.[65] These measures ought also to be taken by those States whose bureaucracies have become detrimental to the common good.

Second, the size of the federal executive ought gradually to be reduced commensurate to the limited scope of its powers and responsibilities envisioned by the Constitution. This process must begin at the highest level of administration: the Cabinet of the United States, which had four officers during the presidency of Washington, and which today has been bloated to fifteen.[66] Such a wide cabinet does not only propagate bureaucracy; it muddles its own ability to advise the

President and that of the President to decide, for a meeting of fifteen rarely yields clear advice. Furthermore, it takes immense time and attention for a President to direct fifteen Cabinet Secretaries; this burden prompts the creation of an extensive White House staff; and the enlarged staff, being comprised of individuals with their own preferences and priorities, takes on a life of its own and wrests the creation of policy from the Cabinet, rendering the Cabinet redundant. Our Union once governed itself with State, Defense, Treasury, Interior, and Justice as its primary departments; it ought to do so again by consolidating other departments within their fold.[67]

Third, discretion in the details of implementing federal laws, whenever possible, ought to be given to the States, and likewise for state laws to local governments. That is to say, in areas such as commerce and health, where it may be necessary and proper that the federal government set standards for the entire Union, it is nonetheless often beneficial that the States decide how best to attain those standards, rather than having their methods prescribed to them by Congress. Doing so would reduce the volume of regulation: for each matter that a subordinate government may decide, the higher government does not need to make a rule. Moreover, local discretion may improve a law's effectiveness by adapting its implementation to local conditions; it also gives ordinary citizens greater ability to influence the process of implementation as conditions change, so as to accomplish the ends of the federal legislation in a way that does the least harm to other objects of public interest.

Moreover, this approach is less likely to violate the non-delegation principle. Whereas Congress must be wary of granting too much discretion to unelected bureaucracies, as doing so may separate lawmaking from the consent of the governed, it may, without reservation, grant discretion in particular matters to the States.[68] State legislatures, like Congress, are representative of the people; legislative authority may be delegated to them without losing the people's consent.

Fourth, as the inevitable effect of reducing the volume of regulations will be to increase the number of controversies brought before the courts, the capacity of the judicial branch ought to be increased so that courts can resolve disputes in a timely and economical manner. We thus call for the federal and state governments to invest in judicial infrastructure, not only in material necessities, such as courthouses, but in human capital as well. Although our Republic is bestowed with an abundance of lawyers, it has too few judges; legislatures at each level of government ought to pass acts providing for governors and the President to appoint a number of new judges each term, over a period of several terms of office, so as to permanently increase the country's stock of judicial officers without the courts being 'packed' by a single executive. In addition, some new courts ought to be dedicated to specific matters formerly guided by regulation, so to ensure wise resolution of cases requiring specialized knowledge.[69] An increase in capacity may also have the salutary effect, by making trial more accessible, of removing lawyers from the backroom and returning them to the courtroom, where they must argue their cases before the public.

Here, however, a word of warning is necessary: legislatures, having ceased to delegate their law-making responsibility to unelected bureaucracies, must not instead yield that duty to unelected judges. The courts exist to arbitrate disputes under the law, not to promulgate the law itself.[70] The sort of judicial activism, common in this era, in which the people look to the courts to issue proclamations that establish, in effect, their preferences into law, must be curtailed. Legislatures, in whose sole hands the legitimate power of crafting laws resides, ought jealously to guard their prerogative from infringement on any side; so too ought the people.[71]

Lastly, as with every great principle, there are practical limitations to the general need for a reduction of the regulatory state. For instance, the safety of food and drugs is clearly a matter of interstate commerce, directly impacts the general welfare, and cannot be specified sufficiently in a concise federal law; the Food and Drug Administration thus ought to retain some regulatory authority. The patron of that agency, Theodore Roosevelt, one of this Republic's most illustrious Presidents and a staunch believer in both free enterprise and the welfare of citizens, was adept in recognizing such circumstances;[72] we regard him as having struck the best balance yet attained between legislative and executive prerogative. Of specific concern to him were competition and conservation, in that the former is necessary to preserve the market by which our Union prospers, and the latter to fulfill our moral obligations as civilized men and women; crucially, neither can be accomplished fully by the States alone. We shall elaborate on these topics in later essays.

A note is warranted on laws regarding general commerce, given that the commerce clause of the Constitution has been much abused to widen the scope of federal legislation, from whence, by the means described above, power usually ends up in the hands of the federal executive.[73] We assert that, to justify a federal law under that clause, the law ought to affect commerce as its main purpose; it ought to regulate activity that is commercial in character, not cite some side-effect it might have on commerce as a pretext to regulate an activity of an entirely different character.[74] If a bill passes that test, Congress ought to make the resulting law clear and predictable, and give sufficient forewarning. For when commercial regulation must occur, it is to the benefit of both business and the public that firms affected understand what to expect and have time to prepare.

It is no simple task to establish principles on the length and complexity of laws at several levels of government, and to recommend how to realize them, within the few pages this format demands. Some intricacies are necessarily omitted. Yet it amounts to this: that, fellow citizens, intrusions of government into your lives and businesses ought to occur as little as possible, and those that must occur ought to be malleable at the level where you may most directly and easily shape them; and that they ought not to be dictated to you from on high, by unelected agencies to whom your representatives surrendered their solemn law-making power. Know, too, that these principles of separation of powers and limited government are not novel concepts, but intended by the Founders of this Union, and by so drawing our Republic back to its origins we can thrive.

No. 5 – On the National Debt

That a national debt is beneficial if maintained at a moderate level – That excessive debt leads to high taxation – That unexpected events can combine with indebtedness to prompt a vicious cycle – That establishing priorities for public spending is the simplest way to manage public debt – That priority ought to be given to defense, diplomacy, infrastructure, research, exploration, and conservation – That discipline ought to be restored to the management of public funds allocated for national defense – That provision for defense and diplomacy accomplishes the same ends – That provision for infrastructure and research is an investment in the future of the Republic

> "Persuaded as the Secretary is, that the proper funding of the present debt, will render it a national blessing: Yet he is so far from acceding to the position, in the latitude in which it is sometimes laid down, that "public debts are public benefits," a position inviting to prodigality, and liable to dangerous abuse, that he ardently wishes to see it incorporated, as a fundamental maxim, in the system of public credit of the United States, that the creation of debt should always be accompanied with

the means of extinguishment. This he regards as the true secret for rendering public credit immortal."
—**Alexander Hamilton, *First Report on Public Credit*, January 9th, 1790.**

In our previous essay, we advocated simplification of federal laws and reduction of the bureaucracy that has accompanied them. We now move our focus to the fuel that gives motion to the vast machinery of government: the public funds. These funds are, in the final reckoning, provided for through taxation, but in the interim they are provided for by government borrowing. This borrowing is the basis of the public debt, known commonly as the national debt.[75] Many of the great questions of state, therefore, regard spending, taxation, and debt. Since the turn of the present century, however, our Republic has failed to reckon with these fiscal matters in a prudent manner. One party calls incessantly for more federal spending; the other vies blindly for the severe reduction of taxes; both approaches inexorably and irresponsibly expand the national debt, which is now strained by the expense of two wars and the retirement of the Baby Boomer generation.[76] Such reckless stoking of the furnace exposes our Union to the caprices of chance and renders it vulnerable to the challenges of its rivals. An errant spark could cause its engine to melt down.

Accepting, as we do, that a well-funded national debt can be in the national interest, so long as it is accompanied by what Mr. Hamilton described as a "means of extinguishment," to be employed if the growth of the debt outstrips the growth of the economy; that excessive taxation impedes prosperity; that taxation is nonetheless necessary for the provision of public goods; and that some public support is warranted to our fellow citizens who, due to twists of fortune, are unable financially to support themselves; we endeavor in the next two essays to present a new approach to taxation and spending, in keeping with the federal structure of our Republic, which shall reinforce the partial sovereignty of the several States, accord choice to citizens, reduce waste, and moderate the national debt. We begin, in this one, with a discussion of the public debt and the rightful priorities for government spending in the discretionary portion of the federal budget. We follow, in the next, with a discussion of the mandatory portion of that budget and of the form and manner of taxation at the federal and state levels of government.

National debt must, like a flame, be considered an essential tool but also a dangerous one, should it escape the control of its user. No sensible person would urge his or her family to forego the use of fire and thus shiver in the cold and dark; so ought no sensible leader to advise his or her fellow citizens to forswear a public debt entirely. Well-funded national debts, which began to be employed by Western nations during the dawning years of the Enlightenment, allow countries that use them to acquire more than they otherwise would have the means to. Just as most private citizens must borrow in order to have, at one time, the capital necessary for purchasing a home, so must governments borrow in order to maintain world-class armies and fleets and to provide public goods for their citizens.[77] And just as the debt that a citizen incurs to purchase a home can, in the long term, prove a profitable investment as the home rises in value, so can government realize long-term gain by borrowing funds to invest, for instance, in infrastructure, wherein the resulting economic growth comes to outweigh the debt incurred. Governments, moreover, have advantages in borrowing that private citizens lack: they exist for several lifetimes, and they have a degree of influence over the market from which they borrow.

Austerity for its own sake thus has little value and holds a nation below its true potential. Nor is the public debt of these United States yet in crisis: the U.S. Government has, since Mr. Hamilton's time, diligently paid its obligations incurred from interest on the public debt, and still does so today; private persons and foreign states thus remain content to lend to our Republic at a manageable cost.[78] Our Union, furthermore, holds a unique position in the world economy, which dampens the incentive for foreign lenders to abruptly call in its debts to them. The U.S. dollar is the world's foremost reserve currency, such that many foreign assets held by creditor nations are denominated in dollars. Should those countries prompt a crisis of payment for the U.S. Treasury, and thereupon a fall in the value of the dollar, they would prompt a fall in their own wealth. It is rare that any country would act against its own interest in such a way; thus has the United States remained so far on solid financial footing despite two decades of profligacy in its expenditure.[79]

That our Republic has benefitted from its public debt so far, however, ought not to lull it into complacency; it should not fall asleep by the fire. All debts must eventually be paid, and taxation is the eventual form of payment for all public debt.[80] This maxim holds true even for that portion of the national debt which is serviced, in effect, for perpetuity; that is, where government pays the interest on the debt at recurring periods while leaving the principal untouched. As the volume of debt accumulates, so does the volume of interest; more government

NO. 5 – ON THE NATIONAL DEBT

revenue must then be dedicated to servicing the interest, and so the volume of taxation steadily increases.

Were the national economy to grow faster than the national debt, it is true, then revenue may increase without the need for an increased rate of taxation.[81] That is often the premise upon which the deceptive species of policy known as the unfunded tax cut and its cousin, the unfunded spending increase, are proposed; but it is a risky gamble. It relies on a prediction of the future, yet the future is difficult to predict. Any unexpected shock, any unforeseen stumble, might slow the economy. If that occurs, the government faces a dilemma. It may restore the higher tax rate, but doing so might slow the economy further, which compounds its difficulties. Or it may double down on its bet by borrowing more funds to service the debt. Doing so throws the public on the mercy of its creditors; at some point, if the prospect of repayment appears remote, and especially if an inviting alternative presents itself, the creditors shall demand higher interest to lend lower sums. Additional borrowing thereby becomes unaffordable; the existing debt must still be serviced; the burden of servicing debt raises taxation, which slows the economy; and reduction in economic growth adds to the difficulty of servicing debt, creating a vicious cycle that may cripple the greatest nations.

History offers a cautionary tale. At the turn of the past century, Great Britain occupied a position similar to that held by these United States today. It had, by means of a long-standing and well-serviced national debt, grown its economy to prosperity, accumulated formidable military might, and extended its influence to all corners of the world. Its banks sat at the center of world finance and its currency led the world onto the gold standard, which gave it value in transactions across the globe. Other nations had little incentive to harm Britain's economy; Britain had little reason to ponder the need for a means of extinguishment to accompany its growing debt.

Then war came. Twice Britain was cast into the center of world war, and each struggle, though it ended with victory, increased the British public debt to a level far beyond the ability of the British government to control.[82] When war subsided, Great Britain found that it was no longer the world's indispensable economy. These United States had grown to take that role; New York came to overshadow London. The rest of the world thus no longer had reason to be lenient with British debt, and so for several decades the people of Britain faced hardship as their government repaid its dues. The British authorities rationed food until 1954; the British Empire collapsed; the British economy did not return fully to life until the 1980s; and when Britain did recover by the century's end, it retained but a shadow of the might and influence it possessed at the start of it.

The expansion of the national debt was not the sole cause of Great Britain's fall from wealth and power,[83] but that it played a key part cannot be denied. Long accustomed to a benign public debt, Britain did not prepare for events that would overwhelm its ability to fund the debt, nor for the possibility that another power might take its place at the world's economic center.[84]

Our Republic ought to note the history of its predecessor. The retirement of the Baby Boomers looms large as an event that could increase its public debt to a height above its control, especially if paired with an unforeseen crisis such as war; and China is advancing as a rival economic power, predicted to overtake these United States in gross domestic product before the middle of this century.[85] China and the European Union, though with limited success so far, also aspire for their currencies to compete with the dollar as an international reserve. Our Union, in order to preserve its position, should thus ready a means of extinguishment, lest the flames of its national debt rise too high and too quickly to contain.

It is beyond the scope of this essay to examine the entire federal budget and prescribe in detail a contingency plan to contain and reduce the public debt; such labor is best left to the two houses of Congress in whom that responsibility is vested. We advance instead the notion that the basic method of readying a means of extinguishment for the national debt is to establish certain priorities for federal spending; then, as the exigencies of state and the market demand, reduce the public debt by diminishing spending in areas that are not accorded priority.[86] Moreover, we favor objects for spending that may be considered investments, and which thereby eventually recoup some of the sum they add to the public debt. Incurring debt for a subsidy, which is merely consumed, offers no such advantage. An individual who takes a loan to study medicine will, in the long run, be better off; one who does so only to lease a sports car will be the worse for wear. So, too, is it with governments that borrow for investments and those that borrow for subsidies.

In this essay, as indicated above, we limit our examination to the 'discretionary' portion of the federal budget, of which the greatest share, by far, is dedicated to those items considered necessary for the common defense. Defense is unmistakably within the proper purview of the federal government, both by the explicit provision of the Constitution and by common logic: the high principles for which this Republic stands will come to naught if these United States lack the means to defend themselves from foreign aggression. We thus endorse without qualm the notion that to be prepared for war is the best means of preserving peace, and liberty.

Yet we do not shrink from declaring that, in recent decades, the Department of Defense, in its management of public funds entrusted to it, has lacked the discipline which characterizes the profession of arms. Instead, it employs perverse and labyrinthine procedures which render impossible the accounting of funds and encourage excessive and ill-considered spending, such that we are willing to wager that the amount spent wastefully by it exceeds the entire budgets of most other federal departments.[87] Once the department fritters away its allocation in this manner, it marches to Congress with open hands, expecting to be given more without thought or scrutiny.

This state of affairs is one that both parties have long indulged, but it is unacceptable in a republic and must be curtailed. It shows contempt for the tax-paying citizen; it instills a sense of entitlement within the defense bureaucracy; and the inefficiency it breeds is counterproductive to military preparedness: small units are overloaded with expensive trinkets, but the Navy lacks ships.[88] The Defense Department ought to receive funds based on military necessity, not merely in comparison to the previous year's budget; it ought to be held accountable through frequent external audits; and it must enact internal reforms that encourage conservation of public funds, rather than profligacy. Only once military discipline is applied to military spending should the citizens of these United States and their representatives in Congress be satisfied.

NO. 5 – ON THE NATIONAL DEBT

There are other items of high importance, and appropriate for federal expenditure, upon which we desire to place greater priority than is presently given. One is diplomacy, in particular the Department of State, which in recent times has been steadily deprived of funds even as its counterpart, Defense, has received ever-greater largesse. That Defense should have a larger share of the federal budget than State is ordinary and acceptable, for the maintenance of armies and fleets requires vast expenditures in equipment and supplies, but it is neither ordinary nor acceptable that increases in defense spending should come at the expense of funds allocated to diplomacy.

Defense and diplomacy are but two sides of the same coin: they serve the same end of sustaining U.S. power abroad, thereby providing security and prosperity at home. A reduction in the diplomatic budget weakens the Republic in the same manner as a reduction in the defense budget; an increase correspondingly strengthens it. The provision of public funds for defense and diplomacy thus ought to rise and fall in tandem, guided by fiscal constraints and the dangers and opportunities that exist abroad. As an interim means of correcting the present imbalance, we propose that funds discovered, upon audit, to have been wastefully allocated by the Department of Defense be first re-apportioned to State, to the amount necessary for all U.S. embassies to perform the full extent of their duties, before being returned to the general fund. Such an approach in the short term would restore our Union's diplomatic capability without necessitating new taxation or additional debt. Thereafter, the proposed budgets for the Departments of State and Defense ought to be presented together to Congress under the title 'Defense and Diplomacy.'

Repair of national infrastructure is another clear and urgent priority, deserving of federal provision because it is important for both the national defense and commerce between the several States. A single levy of federal tax for the purpose of repairing the decay caused by decades of neglect ought to be considered, especially as the economic benefit to be expected from such a repair may eventually offset some or all of the cost in taxation. Thereafter, a new plan ought to be conceived for the regular and continuous maintenance of interstate infrastructure, to be provided for by a re-apportionment of funds from items of lesser urgency in the present federal budget.

The provision of funds for research and development in science, technology, engineering, and medicine ought also to be accorded a high priority in the federal budget. Such development, akin to provisions for infrastructure, ought to be considered a profitable investment in fulfillment of the constitutional duty of Congress to provide for the general welfare and common defense of the United States. Research in medicine provides security to the people of our Republic by better protecting them from the scourge of disease; research in science, technology, and engineering expands the Union's economic potential. Moreover, such research cannot be adequately provided for by private firms or the several States alone. As the returns of research are by their very nature uncertain, commercial entities are at times reluctant to assume the risks and costs of conducting experimentation on their own; nor are the States normally inclined to dedicate many resources to research that might benefit the country substantially, but any one State only marginally.[89]

NO. 5 – ON THE NATIONAL DEBT

There are two more items, related to infrastructure and research, which warrant priority in federal expenditure on account of the fact that they are achievable only by the Union, and that they tend greatly toward the general welfare of these United States. These are the exploration of outer space and the mitigation, halting, and reversal of the global warming phenomenon. Each ought to receive more emphasis and funding than it does at present; but which manner of funding them is most effective, we leave for further debate, our only stipulation being that it ought to be considered in the light of Mr. Hamilton's principle that the national debt be increased only if it is accompanied by a means of extinguishment. The merits of these great tasks, and the means by which they might be accomplished, we shall discuss in detail in a later essay.

Such are the objects that we consider worthy of special priority in the provision of federal funds. In establishing our priorities, we do not imply that no other objects ought to receive funds from the government of these United States. We argue only that, when the need to employ a means of extinguishment for the public debt requires a general reduction in federal expenditure, the objects designated above ought to be preserved to the greatest extent that circumstances allow, whereas other objects may have their provision reduced. We stress, too, that we propose these priorities only for the federal budget; the priorities of the several States do and should differ. We shall now, in our next essay, turn our attention to the mandatory portion of the federal budget, and confront the great questions associated with the provision of welfare contained within.

No. 6 – On Entitlements

That a high amount of federal taxation constrains the partial sovereignty of the States – That all governments owe a minimum of social welfare to their citizens – That the dependence of citizens on government ought to be inversely proportionate to the government's coercive power – That a government's relevance in the eyes of the people depends on the services it provides – That the federal government is a better referee of state debts than of its own – That the federal entitlement system ought to be devolved to the States – That there ought to be federal support to some States for healthcare benefits – That the federal government ought to facilitate movement between States – That pork barrel spending is acceptable within limits – That federal income tax ought to be reduced and a federal sales tax established – That the federal tax code ought to be simplified

> "Indeed the idea of any government existing, in any respect, as an independent one, without any means of support on their own hands, is an absurdity. If therefore, this constitution has in view, what many of its framers and advocates say it has, to secure and guarantee to the separate states the exercise of certain powers of government, it certainly ought to

have left in their hands some sources of revenue."
—'**Brutus**,' *Letter No. 5*, **December 13ᵗʰ, 1787.**

In our previous essay, we examined the benefits and perils of the national debt; we also established certain priorities for spending among the items accounted for in the discretionary portion of the federal budget. In this essay, we shall fix our attention upon the great matters of taxation and welfare which attend the vast social programs contained within the mandatory portion of the federal budget. This system of entitlements, which includes such programs as Social Security, Medicare, and Medicaid, today comprises the lion's share of the budget, but it is in urgent need of reform. Not only is it poised, as the Baby Boomer generation ages, to sink our Republic into the depths of public debt; it also erodes the federal structure of our Union. The taxation required to fund it denies revenue to the States and renders them reliant on federal aid; it overshadows state governments' own efforts to provide for citizens' needs, consigning them to irrelevance in the eyes of their residents; and it renders citizens dangerously dependent upon the federal government for the essentials of life. We seek to offer reforms that reinforce the federal character of these United States and promote their future prosperity and might, while continuing to hold in high regard the obligations of a just government to the welfare of its citizens.

We begin with the principle that federal taxation constrains state taxation. As there exists a natural limit to how much tax may be collected from citizens before economic growth becomes so stunted and evasion so prevalent that revenues decrease,[90] an increase in federal tax necessarily reduces the amount that state and local governments can tax. As federal tax grows, state taxes must correspondingly shrink; state governments are thereby starved of revenue, and then either fall into irrelevance or become dependent upon federal aid, as is the present unfortunate condition of our Union.[91] Thus, a reduction in federal tax is a boon first to the States, which may increase their taxes to fund their own projects. If state legislatures decline to do so, or if they raise their taxes by a lesser amount than that which the federal government has cut, the same opportunity is then passed to local governments; if municipalities similarly decline to raise their taxes, only then does it become a tax cut for businesses or for individual citizens.

Federal spending drives federal taxation; excessive federal spending thereby degrades the partial sovereignty of the several States. It follows that federal spending ought to be moderated. This end is achieved when Congress restrains itself to funding only those functions that are both necessary and proper for the federal government to perform in fulfillment of its enumerated powers. The objects which we identified in our previous essay as deserving of priority in federal spending meet that twofold standard. They are proper because they are either explicitly enumerated in the Constitution to the federal government, or else they fit within the spirit of that founding document; and they are necessary because they cannot be provided for by the States alone. Other functions of government which do not satisfy that standard ought instead to be largely designed, controlled, and funded by the States, or by the municipal governments below them.

We reject the notion, sometimes presented as libertarian, that social welfare, broadly defined as pensions, healthcare, and aid to the poor, ought not to be provided by government in any manner. To take such a line would be to violate the social contract upon which all republics are founded, including our own. All citizens owe something to their government: at a minimum, they may be called to military or civil service in the event of a national crisis. Logically, then, all governments owe something back to their citizens: at a minimum, security, which means a continuous effort to protect the natural lives of citizens. A government that allows its citizens to starve fails to provide security. Thus, the most basic level of welfare – the guarantee of food and other life essentials – is inseparable from even the most limited of just governments. It is also implausible to argue that the provision of welfare by the federal government is strictly unconstitutional: Article 1, Section 8 permits Congress to provide for the "general Welfare of the United States," under which clause the present concept of welfare may certainly be classified. The poor, the sick, and the elderly may not simply be abandoned to their fate.

However, the question herein is whether primary responsibility for welfare is appropriate at the federal level of the United States in accordance with the spirit of the Constitution. To this, we answer broadly in the negative. Rather, our Union ought to apply the principles of federalism to its system of entitlements by devolving its control and upkeep to the lowest practical level of government, which in most cases is the States; and the States, when practical, should delegate portions of their welfare plans to local governments. This determination rests on three principles.

First, in a republic, citizens' dependence on government ought to be in inverse proportion to the coercive force wielded by that government. Government is itself a necessary but fearsome institution.[92] Because mankind is fallible, no government, however well-designed, can be relied upon to remain benign forever; thus at various points in human history it becomes necessary for citizens to resist their government in order to maintain their liberty.[93] Should it become corrupted, the federal government of the United States, whose powerful forces can strike down its enemies even in the remotest regions of the world, cannot be resisted but by the united and determined efforts of a large part of its citizenry. But such popular mobilization in defense of liberty, already difficult in itself, becomes impossible when the people depend upon that government for their basic needs. A citizen, who otherwise loves liberty, will hesitate to raise his voice, or her hand, against a despot who controls his family's access to food or medical care.

A state government, by contrast, possessing militia and police but no formidable army, and moreover being checked, should it become corrupted, by the federal government – which is bound by the Constitution to ensure a republican form of government in all the States[94] – is less threatening to the liberty of its citizens, and opposing it requires less fortitude among them. It is therefore a safer entity for citizens to depend on for subsistence; local governments are safer still.

Second, the federal government's assumption of responsibility for welfare diminishes the relevance of the several States, thereby undermining the constitutional structure of the Republic. For a federal system of government to function well, state and local governments must be seen by their residents to hold important powers and to make decisions that matter to those citizens' lives. If this perception fades, apathy toward local government sets in, and over-centralization begins –

which, in republics, is the first step towards autocracy. If such basic needs as food, pensions, and medical care are provided to citizens by the federal government, there appears to the people no need to mind the governance of their cities and States.

Furthermore, a welfare system requires much taxation; and if that system is enacted at the federal level, it requires much federal taxation. High federal taxation, discussed above, constrains the ability of the States to raise their own revenue and thus hinders their ability to function as partly-sovereign governments. If the several States are given responsibility for the design and support of such systems, however, they shall be reinvigorated with greater purpose and resources.

Third, taxation ultimately funds all systems of welfare, and those systems are established by majority vote. Majority decisions, as we described in previous essays, at times weigh upon those who form the minority in relation to a given vote. This is particularly so for the imposition of taxes. When federal taxes are imposed, all within these United States are bound to accept their burden; but when they are excessive, those persons and firms who pay the most tax are tempted to remove themselves or their assets from the country, causing a loss of revenue to the whole.[95]

Within a single State, however, fewer individuals and interests are involved in legislative decisions, and those which are exist closer to each other, enlarging the possibility of compromise acceptable to a wide section of the population. Moreover, if given discretion, the States will each establish welfare systems of varying generosity and cost, based upon the needs, character, and resources of each State. Citizens who dissent from the scheme adopted by their State may, if they find their situation so intolerable that it outweighs the cost of relocation, move to a different State whose system they find more suitable to their needs or inclinations, yet remain within the Union. Competition between States for business and residents, thus engendered, further increases the incentive of state legislatures to seek compromise and to design an efficient welfare system.

There are also practical benefits to a reform of entitlements that gives control to States. First, state governments are better able to adapt their systems to local needs. If, for instance, Michigan suffered the closing of a major automotive factory, it could adjust its welfare scheme so as to provide specific benefits to workers who lost their livelihoods as a result of that event. The federal government, presiding over a large and diverse territory, cannot react flexibly to particular occurrences. Similarly, state governments, by virtue of having smaller bureaucracies to supervise, can more easily detect and rectify fraud and waste than can the vast federal agencies.

Second, such a devolution would allow the federal government to focus its resources and attention more closely upon those purposes more clearly enumerated to it by the Constitution, in particular those which the federal government alone is able to effectively direct. These purposes, which we outlined in our previous essay, include defense, diplomacy, space exploration, and the halting of global warming. We shall elaborate further on each of those topics in later essays.

Third, if properly implemented, such a reform might serve to moderate the national debt. We base this claim on the premise that the federal government is a more effective referee of the several States than it is of itself. Having long failed to persistently adhere to its own plans for moderating the public debt, Congress may find more lasting success by passing legislation which limits the proportion of debt that state governments may take on to fund their welfare schemes. We believe that such a law could be justified on the precedent, established in 1790 by Alexander Hamilton, of the federal government assuming responsibility for state debts.[96] Such supervision, though it constrains the fiscal autonomy of each State, is a worthy exchange for devolution to the States of the greater power to manage their own entitlement systems. Moreover, any limit on state debt enacted by the federal government might prove unobtrusive. The state governments, by and large, have been better stewards of public funds than their federal counterpart. They do not ordinarily issue bonds except to fund infrastructure, which is likely to provide a return on investment, and all but one have statutes that mandate a balanced budget in some form.[97]

We propose, therefore, that federal entitlement programs which subsidize ordinary costs of living, such as Social Security, food stamps, disability benefits, and direct welfare payments to the poor, be reformed so as to gradually transfer control of their structure and operation, as well as responsibility for their funding, to the several States. The funds necessary to achieve this end would be made available to the States through a general reduction of federal tax, which, in keeping with the principle described in the first part of this essay, shall enable the States to increase their own taxation by a corresponding amount.

The attentive and critical reader shall here jump to point out that this reform, along with several of our previous proposals tending toward greater political responsibility and fiscal self-reliance for the States, shall have the consequence of exposing economic inequalities between them. The welfare services provided by the government of Alabama, for instance, might be more constrained by budgetary necessity than those of the government of California.

That charge is true. An inescapable consequence of devolution to the States is that not all state governments will be able to provide their residents benefits equal to those enjoyed in other States, since the several States have varying economic capacities. In response, we say first that these differences in the economic fortunes of states are an unavoidable part of a federal system, which occur naturally and persist whether or not they are papered over by the national government. The federal government, moreover, possessing at present a vast and unresponsive bureaucracy, does a poor job at papering them. That bureaucracy already sets the amounts it pays for Social Security and other benefits by region, supposedly in accordance with circumstances in those areas, but it makes adjustments slowly and not always accurately. Devolving responsibility to the States shall make that process automatic and more aligned with economic reality.

Second, the natural divergence in fortunes between States does no injustice to individual citizens in the case of pensions and the other benefits mentioned above, because those entitlements serve to subsidize the cost of living, and the cost of living varies by State. Oklahoma, for instance, may not be able to provide its residents with a pension equal, in dollar terms, to that provided by New York; but that fact does no harm to Oklahomans' livelihoods, because the price of rent in Tulsa is only a fraction of what it is in New York City.

Programs providing medical assistance, such as Medicare and Medicaid, present a different set of considerations and

NO. 6 – ON ENTITLEMENTS

thus a somewhat different solution. The cost of healthcare varies less by region than does the ordinary cost of living, for the industry that supplies drugs and medical equipment serves a national market and does not have an independent presence in every State. A full devolution of existing federal healthcare benefits would thus result in the residents of some States being less able to afford care than residents of other States, or it might result in a lower quality of care being available to citizens who rely on government benefits in those States. Such inequality between States, in providing for the health of citizens who cannot provide for themselves, may be considered a failure to provide equally for those citizens' security; it thus ought not to be ignored by a Union that guarantees to its citizens the inalienable rights of life and equality before the law. We thus propose only a partial devolution of federal healthcare schemes to the States, which shall give the several States discretion over those systems' design, but in which the federal government shall also disburse grants to supplement the funds of States whose per capita income is below the Union's median.[98]

Some will decry our proposed reforms of welfare and healthcare as disrupting the lives of those who, at the moment, depend on the existing federal benefits, or as upending the fortunes of those who, for their entire lives, expected to receive Social Security pensions and planned their finances accordingly. It is not our intent for those citizens to be left stranded by a change in legislation. The shift must therefore occur over a time period sufficient for individual citizens to adjust their plans in accordance with it; the federal government must not relinquish control until the various state plans have been resolved upon and enacted; and, as regards pensions, those who have already paid taxes into the current scheme ought to retain benefits in proportion to the amount they have already contributed.[99] Such safeguards, we trust, shall satisfy the sensible majority who understand the necessity of reform yet must also provide for themselves and their families during the period of transition.

Others will assert that firms and individuals will take advantage of reform. Firms, they fear, will move assets to those States which have the least generous welfare systems and thus the lowest rate of taxation, thereby forcing other States to reduce their welfare systems as well. Yet such an effect, even were it to occur, seems preferable to the prevailing one, in which firms move their assets abroad and leave the federal government with a welfare system that it cannot sustain. Nor, at any rate, would it be a permanent effect: if enough firms flee to a low-tax State, the wealth and population of that State will grow until it, too, demands more for its people. Even that effect is likely to be small, however. Many firms linger in high-tax States today for reasons such as proximity to cities and infrastructure, which will remain considerations tomorrow.

Moving, moreover, is not the domain of the rich alone, nor ought it to be. A fundamental advantage to this proposed reform is that it provides a spur for ordinary citizens to move to areas of growing economic productivity, where they may find gainful employment, rather than eke out a bare living on federal subsidies in areas whose economic capacity is not expanding fast enough to employ them. The Constitution grants all citizens of the United States the right to move freely between the several States and hold all the privileges of citizenship in each.[100] Citizens who are unsatisfied with their economic situation in the State where they reside have a free choice: they may remain, inspired by love of home to forego opportunities or services they might obtain by moving; or they may move, and so follow the enterprising spirit of their forebears who first left the Old World for the New. Yet this advantage is only realized if citizens can afford the cost of relocation. We thus propose that the federal government offer a benefit, which may be claimed a few times in each citizen's life, to reimburse a move between States.[101]

Movement of citizens between States shall rebalance the population of each in proportion to its resources: in a State with few resources, those who remain are left with a greater share. The prospect of gaining or losing population shall also spur competition among States, and inspire compromises within them, to provide public services and economic opportunities for residents. Such a contest, properly regulated by the federal government under its authority to supervise commerce between States, tends toward the prosperity of the Union. Thus, over time, stripping away the thin screen of federal subsidies might increase the per capita wealth of all the States.

Individuals, our critics will say, may abuse their freedom of movement by living in States with low welfare when they are young and working, then moving to States with high welfare on retirement, or if injured, despite having not contributed to those States' revenues before. Such fear is also exaggerated, especially in this disruptive economic era: as forces such as automation make an unbroken career more difficult to attain, even the young and vigorous might see wisdom in residing in a State that offers adequate welfare provisions. Yet state and federal action can also discourage gamesmanship. Those States that maintain generous pensions could introduce laws, in which the benefit a resident receives is in proportion to length of residency and contribution made to the state revenue; and the federal government could oversee the transfer and conversion of a citizen's paid, but yet unused benefits from one State to another upon that citizen's move.

Finally, some will charge that our proposed reform will lose some measure of economic efficiency derived from a welfare system of federal scale. We accept that charge; we believe that it will be mitigated in part by gains from interstate competition; and we at any rate consider it to be well worth the value the reform shall bring by strengthening our Republic's federal structure.

We must also briefly discuss the method of taxation that shall make such reform possible. Limiting the amount of federal tax is not itself sufficient to assure revenue to the States; it is best for the federal and state governments to collect taxes in different ways, so as not to exhaust the same source of revenue.[102] In the early years of Union, the federal government drew revenue from duties and imposts, particularly on non-essential goods, whereas the States taxed income.[103] After the 16th Amendment authorized the federal income tax in 1913, methods shifted: the federal government now collects revenue principally from income, whereas many state governments rely upon sales taxes. We do not propose that the 16th Amendment be repealed, as events might arise which require the federal government to draw from that source of revenue.[104] We do propose that, commensurate to our proposed welfare reform, these modes be rebalanced in practice: that States tax a greater share of income, whereas federal income tax rates be correspondingly reduced; and that Congress enact a federal sales tax, which shall supersede the various state sales taxes, on a variety of items not necessary for the sustenance of life.

There are four arguments for such a reform. First, in purely practical terms, income taxes generate the most revenue compared to other forms of taxation. If the States are to take on the burden of entitlements, which comprise the largest share of federal spending at present, it is logical that they ought to increase their share of the most productive form of taxation. Second, the use of the revenue would fit the means of collecting it. Welfare systems are meant to ease the hardships of citizens who are unable to support themselves; as those citizens are the recipient, they cannot also in any substantial manner be the provider. Income taxes are generally of a progressive nature, in which those who have more wealth pay more tax than those who have less; they are thus a fitting means of providing for entitlements. The objects we propose to leave to the federal government, such as national defense, affect all equally and thus are the equal responsibility of all. Sales taxes are undiscerning of wealth, and thus fit for these purposes; all pay an equal rate.

Third, such a reform reinforces the federal structure of our Republic. Citizens are willing to pay tax because they see the benefit that returns from it.[105] If the States assume greater responsibilities affecting the lives of citizens, it is fitting that they collect taxes most directly. Sales taxes, by contrast, are less direct and thus less onerous to citizens.[106] Moreover, if well-crafted, they provide the citizen an element of choice: those who consume more goods pay more tax.[107] It is appropriate for the federal government, whose ends are less tangible to the people, to tax in a less intrusive manner. Fourth, a uniform sales tax is conducive to commerce: firms shall have to calculate only the effect of a single rate when pricing their goods throughout the Union.

In addition, a simplification of federal tax law would nurture federalism, among myriad other boons. The endless scattering of tax incentives and penalties presently in existence enables the federal government to meddle, using financial means, in the decisions of citizens, businesses, and lower levels of government alike. Recent efforts at tax reform, though successful in reducing rates, have failed to reckon fully with these maddening complexities. We therefore propose that Congress once more revise the federal tax code to remove loopholes, incentives, and penalties, and reduce the rate of taxation in proportion to the increase in revenue brought by simplification.

Finally, it is a crucial facet of our Republic's federal structure that any shift in population and revenue between States, the natural occurrence of which might be accelerated by the reforms to taxation and welfare proposed in this essay, shall have its ill effects mitigated by the equal representation of all States in the Senate. This scheme of representation ensures that even those States with sparse populations and small revenues may not be sidelined in the apportionment of such federal resources as are appropriately disbursed. Consequently, efforts by members of Congress to situate federal projects within their States – vilified in the past two decades as 'pork-barrel spending' – ought not to be prohibited. 'Pork-barrel' projects provide a countervailing force to the divergences noted above. Each State ought to derive benefit from membership in the Union; it is natural for representatives to seek benefit for their State; and it is healthy for citizens to see their representatives working on their behalf

NO. 6 – ON ENTITLEMENTS

and to perceive those tangible benefits of Union, so long as the projects concerned are appropriate for federal spending and not injurious to the fiscal position of the Republic.

We venture to assert that these proposed reforms, taken together and unfolded gradually, shall shore up the federal foundation of our Republic, help restore it to fiscal health, and provide choice to citizens while nonetheless honoring their government's obligations to them. Having thus envisioned a federal structure for taxation and spending, we shall now, in our next essay, turn to the strategies that governments at all levels may employ to maintain these United States of America as that which their reputation demands: a land of opportunity.

No. 7 – On Economic Inequality

That severe economic inequality can produce ill effects in a republic – That opportunity is more desirable than equality – That competition provides the basis for opportunity – That government may regulate the market in certain ways – That government ought to invest in public goods, not subsidize poverty – That antitrust laws ought to be updated and enforced – That federal oversight of commercial finance is indispensable – That there ought to be competition between public and private education – That public education ought to be made competitive – That public provision for healthcare may be made by the States, and private insurance ought to compete freely with it – That governments ought to make investments which ease the cost of housing and transport

"The credit belongs to the man who is actually in the arena, whose face is marred by dust and sweat and blood; who strives valiantly; who errs, who comes short again and again, because there is no effort without error and shortcoming; but who does actually strive to do the deeds; who knows great enthusiasms, the great devotions; who spends himself in a worthy cause; who at the best knows in the end the triumph of high achievement, and who

NO. 7 – ON ECONOMIC INEQUALITY

at the worst, if he fails, at least fails while daring greatly, so that his place shall never be with those cold and timid souls who neither know victory nor defeat." **—Theodore Roosevelt, "Citizenship in a Republic" speech, April 23rd, 1910.**

In our previous essay, we argued for the rebalancing of fiscal responsibilities between the federal government and the several States so as to preserve the structure of our Union. Having so examined the wealth of the Republic, we shall now address the wealth of its citizens, which has in recent times undergone a great divergence.[108] Economic inequality is an inescapable subject in this 21st century, and it is one which regularly attracts an array of deluded and harmful proposals. Such notions as the nationalization of banks and industry, peddled by the salesmen of illiberal democracy in its leftward manifestation, serve no end but to erode the right of property and spirit of enterprise upon which American prosperity is founded. We offer instead that the system of free markets remains the best means, as it has always been, to generate wealth for the Republic and opportunity for its citizens; that it fails to do so when the competition underlying that system is hindered; and that competition ought to be structured so that citizens can recover when they stumble, and return to the fray with new purpose and vigor.

Economic inequality among citizens demands separate consideration from the inequality among states that is a natural part of a federal republic. Should a vast divergence in individual fortunes become both widespread and insurmountable, it is not only a failure to fulfill that central promise of American citizenship, an opportunity for a prosperous life; it also becomes toxic to liberty. It corrodes freedom by heightening the allure of extreme measures, proposed with the ostensible end of tearing down inequality, that play on the jealousies of citizens.[109] When enough people struggle to meet the necessities of life and see among themselves a few whose riches are both spectacular and unreachable, their reason leaves them, passion takes over, and they consent to demagogic schemes with disastrous result. Communism appealed to Russian farmers and workers because they, desperately poor, gazed at the opulence of the Czarist nobility, which they could never hope to equal. If a republic should reach such a state of affairs, its liberty is doomed.

It follows, therefore, that even those citizens of these United States whose present wealth allows them to live comfortably, and who justly desire to uphold the right of property, have a strong interest in tempering the ill effects of inequality. It is better to do so proactively and moderately, than to ignore the grievances of the less fortunate until a despot emerges and embarks upon a path of pillage and repression, which serves nobody and ravages the Republic.

Yet the instinctive response to the harmful effects of great economic inequality – to push for great equality – leads its advocates dangerously astray. There is always tension in republics between equality and liberty. Equality before the law is necessary for and reinforces political liberty; it is legal equality that the Declaration of Independence upholds. But equality before the law is wrongly conflated with economic equality. Whereas some convergence in fortunes may help to maintain freedom by dampening the appeal of illiberal temptations, strict pursuit of such equality instead undermines liberty and the republican government that liberty preserves.[110]

Differences of talent and temperament between citizens naturally produce differences of fortunes; to equalize those fortunes requires the state to seize what some citizens have privately earned; this act produces resistance; resistance prompts repression. Appropriation also engenders apathy, for the individual no longer sees a reward for his or her work; apathy permits usurpation of political power by tyrants.[111] Communism had economic equality as its principal goal; mankind witnessed it inflict unspeakable brutality, then fail. Strict economic equality is therefore neither achievable nor desirable. It is better to seek the old American promise of equality of opportunity, wherein each citizen may pursue prosperity and have a fighting chance of attaining it.

We must therefore counter the loss of opportunity; and we must redress the cause, not merely patch up the symptoms. The simplistic approach, often presented, of stripping the rich of wealth through excessive taxation and then redistributing that wealth in the form of handouts or subsidies, is both unprincipled and inadequate. It is unprincipled because it is a thinly-veiled assault upon the right of property. It is inadequate because, in the words of the famous proverb, it hands a man a fish, only feeding him for a day, rather than teaching him how to fish, feeding him for life. The opportunity to prosper comes about because of free enterprise; free enterprise, in turn, thrives on competition.[112]

The free market may be likened to Mr. Roosevelt's arena: competition inside it, properly structured, benefits not only entrepreneurs, but all citizens. Competition for workers creates jobs and increases wages; competition for sales lowers prices; competition for customers improves services. Rather than subsidize poverty, our Republic ought to invest in opportunity by enabling competition to occur and its citizens to compete – again and again until they prosper.

In most instances, competition is fostered by low regulation, light taxation, and the absence of government interference in the market, as we argued in previous essays. Yet capitalism is not an end in itself, but the best means to achieve one: the prosperity of the Republic and its citizens. A free market does not exist in anarchy, nor should it. Anarchic capitalism leads only to its own destruction through excessive speculation or the creation of monopolies, like a storm that, by the intensity of its downpour, soon exhausts itself. Finance is to enterprise what water is to life, but rampant speculation sucks the reservoir dry and leaves a desert in its wake. Competition is the current of capitalism, but monopolies and cartels dam the river's flow and flood its banks. It follows, then, that the economy of a government which never regulates the market shall suffer the same misfortunes as a government which does so too frequently.[113]

Some government oversight of the market is therefore a necessity, but government ought first to structure the market rather than intervene in it; and when it must intervene, it ought only to do so in order to maintain competition. Consider, as a basic matter, how the Constitution itself provides for the enforcement of contracts, bankruptcy law, and the establishment of patents, all of which are government functions that are vital to the conduct of business.[114] In keeping with this spirit, we present three general ways in which government may justly facilitate competition.

The first is to impede the entrenchment of monopolies and cartels that, although produced by the free market, serve once established to suppress competition. To do so effectively in these modern times requires a new model of antitrust policy which does not rely on the simple tactic of dismantlement employed by the trust-busters of old. The market today, characterized by vast networks that span the world and shift about in the blink of an eye, quickly amplifies success and swiftly punishes failure. Champions rise to dominate the arena, but may be toppled in their turn. It is true also that the rapid and worldwide flow of information which can nourish a behemoth may instead, or even concurrently, sustain a myriad of microscopic firms which can compete with their globe-spanning brethren, if not in their whole business, then at least in part of it. In this way, a giant can be kept in check by a horde of mice. The consequence of both phenomena is that it is rare for many fighters of the same weight and stature to pace the ring at one time.

It would thus be counterproductive for antitrust action today to focus on breaking large firms into several parts of similar size. In place of trust-busting, we suggest instead a policy of trust-exercising. Emphasis ought to be placed on keeping the giants lean, and thereby unable to suffocate the market by raising prices and depressing wages. Such firms become fat and indolent either when there are not enough small competitors to occupy them on all sides, or when those competitors have no prospect of growing large enough to disrupt the incumbent's grip. These situations may arise when a firm or group of firms has expanded horizontally so far as to control virtually the entire market for one good or service, or when a firm that has become massive through vertical expansion accumulates enough capital that it can simply purchase any aspiring competitor nearly as soon as that challenger is conceived.

The market cannot by itself eliminate these indolent giants until they grow so slothful as to become altogether inert. In the intervening time, however, they will have held their industry in a state of distortion that diminishes its growth and thereby reduces opportunity for citizens.[115] It is not within the power of the several States to remedy this state of affairs, for the nature of a monopoly in a federal republic is such that it transcends state boundaries. It is thus necessary and proper in such circumstances for the federal government to prosecute anti-competitive mergers and acquisitions under antitrust law.

Some modern firms argue that they could not effectively provide their product without economies of a massive horizontal scale, and that such 'network effects' preclude them from having competitors of any size. In this instance, if the good or service they provide is purely a luxury, they must perhaps be left to their own monopolistic devices. If instead it may rationally be considered something that is essential to the public, then the firm ought to be regulated in some way, akin to providers of utilities such as water and electricity. The purpose of government oversight in most such instances, however, is to ensure that those firms shall not excessively raise prices or otherwise deprive citizens of the public good that they provide, and nothing more.

The second general way in which government may foster competition is to pass structural legislation to prevent financial speculation on a self-destructive scale, insofar as such laws follow to the furthest extent practical the principle of non-delegation of legislative power to regulatory agencies. Also, if compelled by circumstance, the federal government may justly respond to a market crash by means of direct fiscal intervention.[116] The largest commercial banks are as far beyond the control of state governments as are the fattest monopolies; and if they fail as a result of uncontrolled speculation, they destroy not only themselves but countless other firms, and damage the national economy.[117]

The third way is to invest in public goods and services (we use the term 'public good' hereafter to refer to both) which, as they are available to all citizens and facilitate enterprise, are crucial to creating opportunity. The means by which this end is pursued, moreover, are decisive to its outcome. Governments often swing between entirely public provision of such goods and full privatization; both methods lack competition and thus efficacy. When the government lacks the will or ability to do a job itself, and therefore fully privatizes that function, there is some competition among individual contractors, but no bottom line that all contractors must compete against; they often extract near-unlimited public funds to complete the task once begun, and their work may be of lesser quality than that done by government. Instead, the government ought to remain in the arena, but allow private firms to compete with it to provide the public good.

Such partial privatization forces the firms to provide the good more efficiently than the government does in order to remain in business; with services, it gives citizens a choice of a cheap but cumbersome public option or a costly but efficient private one. Consider the example of parcel delivery. Citizens may send packages cheaply via the U.S. Postal Service, or buy faster service from a company such as UPS or FedEx. Those two firms, in addition to competing with each other, must ensure that their services are more efficient than those of the Postal Service, or else they would have no reason to exist.

Most citizens will, at various times, use both those firms and the Postal Service, depending on the occasion; by having such a choice, the citizen benefits.

We shall now incorporate those general methods into practical proposals which are more akin to Theodore Roosevelt's Square Deal than the New Deal of Franklin Roosevelt, insofar as they shall create opportunity by fostering competition, and, through competition, improve public services, rather than merely redistribute wealth through high taxation. Theodore Roosevelt urged his fellow citizens to compete; he knew that they would sometimes win and sometimes lose; but he had faith that, if they had the courage to seize the chance before them, they would ultimately prosper.[118] Our proposals, though by no means exhaustive, are meant to create opportunities for all citizens of our Republic by addressing present difficulties in five areas: antitrust, finance, education, healthcare, and mobility.

First, Congress ought to revise existing antitrust legislation to address those aspects of the modern market which we described above, as well as particular manifestations of monopoly that arise therein. One such manifestation is the dominance some firms enjoy in the intangible market for mass repositories of data, which they hoard so as to deny potential competitors the essential nutrient for growth in online commerce.[119] Another, common in this internet age, is when a firm creates, nearly single-handedly, an entirely new marketplace, and then uses this unique position to become both the steward of the new market and the dominant vendor within it. Such a company, as the just reward for its ingenuity, deserves for a time the fruits of the former role; but its foray into the latter suffocates competition and thus ought to be limited.

Yet, as we have noted, countering monopolistic practices today by simplistically breaking the offender into several independent entities tends to cause inefficiency in the market and rarely offers benefit to citizens. Instead, a revised law ought to facilitate prosecution of anti-competitive mergers and acquisitions. Particular provision ought to be made so as to limit industry giants' horizontal acquisitions of small, 'startup' firms. Such firms, as they have the potential either to grow and compete generally with the incumbents, or to remain small and compete locally, hold the key to keeping the large trusts well-exercised and thereby serving the interests of citizens.

As the laws are revised, antitrust suits ought to be pursued rigorously in the federal courts when appropriate criteria are met.[120] Such cases ought not to be settled by feeble half-measures such as issuing fines to offending firms, for they can easily pay such levies; nor by extracting empty promises, in which those firms glibly proclaim that they shall not raise prices nor depress wages. No such vow can be trusted, because, like the scorpion in the fable, it is the nature of a monopoly to do such things,[121] and if an acquisition allows a firm to behave as a monopoly, that nature shall sooner or later emerge. The case, if it was raised on legitimate grounds, ought to be pursued to its conclusion in a court verdict, or else ended by the firm withdrawing its bid.

Such prosecutions ought not, however, to be used merely to shield favored firms, whose failure to compete is entirely of their own doing; and under no circumstances ought antitrust laws to be used to ransack private firms and replace them with ones run by or connected to the state, as is the practice in

Moscow and Beijing. Rather, they ought to protect the citizen, whose cost of living rises as a result of monopolistic practices, and the Republic, whose economic potential goes unrealized when monopolies restrict enterprise and opportunity to a handful of channels.

Of particular concern, however, are 'information monopolies,' whose arbitrary influence over the news that citizens obtain, and over the interactions they have with their fellow citizens, conflicts with the principles of liberty. We consider these firms to be providing a public good, in the shape of a public forum, and thus to be in need of government oversight. We propose that the First Amendment protection of free speech be extended to those customers who are U.S. citizens or subject to U.S. jurisdiction, so that the firms may not restrict those individuals' expressions except in accordance with U.S. law; that simple standards for transparency be established, namely that country and company of origin be disclosed on advertisements and user accounts; and that safeguards for privacy in personal data be established. We believe that these measures, if well calibrated, shall be sufficient, and no further intervention in those businesses is warranted.

The spirit of trust-busting extends also to ending government monopolies on public goods and allowing partial privatization in the manner described above. However, the government, at all levels, ought to maintain a monopoly on the use of force.[122] Private armies and police forces are a threat to liberty and a source of embarrassment for our Republic, whether they are employed domestically or abroad. Only elected governments, whether local, state, or federal, are representative of the people and vested with their will. Thus, the lawful right of force, except in instances of personal self-defense, is vested only in those governments, and in no other entity.

Second, the status quo in regard to government oversight of commercial finance ought to be upheld. The Dodd-Frank Act, passed after the crisis of 2008, has, through its establishment of capital reserve requirements and routine testing of the largest banks, prevented thus far a return to the speculative practices that caused the great crash. That Act's modification by the recent Congress, in raising the size threshold for banks which must submit to the Act's most stringent limitations, tends to the public good by allowing smaller banks to take some risks to compete and grow, in the understanding that, if they fail, they do not possess the weight to take the Republic's economy in tow. We propose only that this Act continue at intervals to be reviewed by Congress, so that the regulatory authority it bestows may not someday exceed the intent of the law.

Third, the several state governments ought to permit and encourage competition between public, charter, and private schools. Education is the foundation of enterprise and much else, and competition can strengthen it. Competition should occur in all districts: charter schools ought not to be placed selectively so as leave to poor communities the option of public schools alone. States and counties ought also to make their public schools competitive by raising the pay of teachers, so as to attract talent to that career; by linking a portion of that pay to performance; and by dismissing teachers who consistently fail to perform, since their failure causes the failure of their pupils.[123] Furthermore, the federal government, acting under its power to regulate commerce between States, ought to create an exacting standard for completion of secondary education, in the form of an examination, leaving to state and local governments exclusive power to design curriculums. Such an act shall prompt competition between teachers, schools, and governments, and give firms a clear assessment of the educational attainment of potential employees.[124]

Higher education demands a different set of proposals. Much has been made, and rightly, of the unreachable price of a modern university education. Yet the cost of college is a result of supply and demand, and tuition subsidies cannot rectify it. Demand is high due to a pervasive belief that every citizen should attend college, which has led to a proliferation of economically valueless degrees and a lack of skilled tradesmen. If trade certifications can compete with four-year degrees in availability and in their potential to offer a prosperous life to citizens, demand for degrees will fall, and so will their cost. State governments thus ought to invest in the quality of public universities relative to their private counterparts and also incorporate trade certification programs into those institutions, as many community colleges have already done.

Fourth, the cost of healthcare ought to be reduced, first by restoring a competitive market for medical services, and then by investment from state governments in public health. A citizen, whose energies are drained by illness and whose finances are drained by the cost of treatment, is in no position to seize an opportunity that comes his or her way. Yet the nationalization of health care, like the nationalization of other industries, is an alluring slogan but a false solution. The call for a single-payer system at the federal level is a call for monopsony – a market in which there is only one buyer – which is merely the other side of monopoly.[125] The rules of the market are similarly disregarded therein, and the result made worse by the fact that the sole buyer is an inefficient bureaucracy which may add freely to the public debt. In any such system, costs will be high – hidden, in this case, in the form of high taxation – and services will be poor. If we are to regard healthcare as a human right, nationalization is a lackluster means of ensuring it.

Nonetheless, critics of the present system shall point out, rightly, that it is hardly itself an efficient one. That charge is true because the existing system is not a fully competitive market, but a half-measure between free enterprise and central control. The federal government, by virtue of its vast Medicare system, exercises a considerable degree of monopsony power over the medical market. It thus behaves as a monopsony does, by fixing the prices it is willing to pay through Medicare for certain procedures. These set prices distort the market. As they force health care providers to take a loss on some procedures, those providers must then inflate the price of other services to compensate for their losses, such that few aspects of care are priced according to their value. Common procedures may become expensive, while rare ones may become cheap; such is the confusion and inefficiency brought by a lack of competition. We thus propose that the federal government eliminate its pricing schedule and thereby restore the market to balance.

Yet removing the federal government's monopsony, and its accompanying fixed prices, shall only go so far in reducing the cost of care to accessible levels. The remainder must be done by the States.[126] State governments ought first, in keeping with the principle of investment before subsidy, to invest substantially in public health infrastructure. There is, at present, a shortage of public hospitals and clinics throughout the Union; the States ought to set aside funds to build and maintain these. There is also a shortfall of nurses; state legislatures can expand nursing schools at state universities and dedicate scholarship funds for those who attend them. Such investments here and there shall have the effect of further reducing healthcare costs by bolstering supply.

If, despite those measures, a gap still persists between the cost of care and what citizens can afford, then it is the prerogative of state governments, if a majority in their legislatures so vote, to offer subsidized health plans to their residents. Should a State do so, it ought also to allow private insurers to compete against it, thereby gaining the benefits of partial privatization described above.[127] Such public plans, offered by the States, carry fewer drawbacks than a federal one. As there are fifty States, and the healthcare industry is national, no State shall exert the monopsony power that the federal government can; and as not all States shall opt to subsidize to a high degree, private insurers shall be able to remain competitive in the overall market. Thus, in stages, can the challenge of healthcare be reckoned with in a manner that works in concert with the forces of the free market and the founding principles of these United States.

Fifth, citizens must be able to move in pursuit of opportunity. The act of moving entails expenses that fall generally into the categories of housing and transport. The federal government, as we proposed in earlier essays, ought to assist by providing each citizen a credit to be applied toward the cost of relocation and by investing in infrastructure, such as interstate highways and rail systems, that reduces the cost of transport. State and local governments, for their part, ought to ease zoning regulations and other restrictions that impede construction of new residences in urban and suburban areas, thus increasing the supply of homes and making them more affordable to citizens. States can also reduce certain administrative fees, such as those for registering a vehicle.

Envision, fellow citizens, a renewed model of capitalism, based on honest, vigorous, and fair competition, in which opportunity is made accessible to all without diminishing the liberty of any; in which each citizen may, if he or she works for it, attain a share of the common wealth, while still allowing that wealth to grow. The American Dream may never be quite perfect; it may never be fully attained; but we must work toward it nonetheless, while maintaining the right of property and system of free markets that have time and again brought prosperity to our Union. Our countrymen have seen hard times before, and overcame them; we shall do the same.

No. 8 – On Trade

That these United States ought to champion free trade – That global trade is irreversible and ought to be seized as an opportunity – That tariffs function as a regressive tax – That trade strengthens our Republic's foreign relations – That protectionism cannot restore jobs, but competition shall – That the United States ought to rejoin the Trans-Pacific Partnership and conclude other trade agreements – That state and local governments ought to invest in ways to train workers and alleviate temporary unemployment – That limited anti-dumping measures are appropriate to counter excess supply – That our Republic and its allies ought to challenge countries which employ anti-competitive trade practices – That automated systems ought to have human supervision – That some protection must exist for industries vital to the national defense

> "I have also had an opportunity of marking from day to day the effect upon great social interests of freedom of trade and comparative abundance... and I am led to the conclusion that the main grounds of public policy on which protection has been defended are not tenable... It is now impossible for us, after we see the results of the change in the Tariff during the last four years, to contend that protection to

industry is in itself, and abstractedly, a public good."
—Sir Robert Peel's speech to the British Parliament on the repeal of the Corn Laws, January 22nd, 1846.

In our previous essay, we examined economic exchanges between citizens and firms and how broader prosperity may be attained by encouraging competition within these United States. In this essay, we shall devote our attention to economic relations between our Union and the rest of the world, and how they, too, may bring prosperity through open and vigorous competition; that is, by free trade. The false prophets of illiberal democracy, on both left and right, have lately taken to undermining the confidence of their fellow citizens and dulling their enterprising spirit with soothing talk of 'protection.' Those words have been followed by actions, such as the precipitate withdrawal of our Republic from trade agreements and the indiscriminate imposition of tariffs, which have encumbered the economy at home and diminished our Union's prestige abroad. We contend that protectionism does not protect, but rather places a burdensome tax upon the citizens of our Republic and threatens the national interests of these United States. Americans ought instead to step back into the arena of free trade; they must summon the will to compete; and their government ought then to contribute tools and training with which they may thrive.

An astute reader might note that in this series we have drawn extensively from the works of Alexander Hamilton, the first Secretary of the Treasury, and that Hamilton is remembered for instituting a system of tariffs intended to develop American industry. That he did so is true, and his reasons then were sound, but they were particular to the situation of these United States in 1791, when our Republic was yet small and undeveloped. We assert that our Union today ought instead to be likened to Great Britain in 1846: industrial, wealthy, and pre-eminent among the great powers. In that year, the British Parliament debated and repealed the Corn Law tariffs, and the British then bore the standard of free trade into the zenith of their history. We argue that the best years of our own Republic, too, are still ahead of it, but that their attainment depends upon the decisions we as citizens now make; and that among these is the continuance of free trade.

To this end, we must begin by examining the origins and nature of trade. We first assume that man, in civilization, cannot alone produce everything that he requires; indeed, if he tried, his own production and sustenance would suffer by attempting it, because he would have to divert his labor away from the things that he routinely and effectively produces.[128] Man therefore trades with his neighbor to obtain the items he lacks, since it may happen that a neighbor has dedicated more time and effort to obtain a certain item, or is more skillful in crafting it, or happens to live on a plot of land where that item is more easily produced. From there, it takes only a few steps of logic to reach world trade: towns trade with each other for the same reasons as individuals; cities for the same reasons as towns; and countries for the same reasons as cities.[129]

This understanding of the origins of trade leads us to two conclusions. First, trade occurs naturally to mankind at all levels of society.[130] Second, its only natural barrier is in the difficulty of communication and transport between places where mankind has settled; thus, global trade is the logical and inevitable result of improvements in communication and transport between countries. Attempts to obstruct world trade are therefore arbitrary and artificial, and as the tendency of arbitrary interference in the natural workings of a free market is to create loss and inefficiency, so is it the case with tariffs. Trade, in other words, is an inexorable part of human progress, and to resist it is often both harmful and futile; better, then, to seize the opportunities it offers.

For while trade is largely inevitable, it is also mostly beneficial. It permits specialization, or division of labor, which increases production by allowing each person, town, or country to focus their efforts on the good or service that they can most effectively provide.[131] It also enables logistical flexibility: some items are best produced near a source of raw materials, for instance, or are more economically transported by sea than by land. Free trade allows the producers and consumers of goods to scour the world to satisfy such considerations. Confined to a town, their scope is limited; confined to a country, it is larger; opened to the world, it is enormous.

Greater scope and flexibility beget greater efficiency. Efficiency is manifest in the global supply chain, wherein goods may be produced by the people best equipped to produce them in the location best suited for their production, then sold in the place with the greatest demand for them. The parts of a refrigerator may be manufactured in China, Canada, and Texas; those parts assembled in Mexico; and the final product sold in New York. Such efficiency results in reduced prices: the refrigerator, assembled in Mexico, sells in New York for fifty dollars less than it would if it were instead assembled there. The reduced price of goods, in turn, reduces the cost of living in the place where the goods are sold; money thus saved is spent on other goods, creating demand; and profits made by the producer from manufacturing goods efficiently are invested in additional productive capacity or in other enterprises, bolstering supply. Economic growth, whose basis is supply and demand, thus occurs in all places that take part in trade, whether by producing an item or by purchasing it. The opposite effect results from protection: the price of goods, and thus the cost of living, rises; savings and investment fall; and growth slows. Tariffs therefore insidiously take the form of a regressive tax.[132]

It must be also noted that trade has a salutary effect on relations between countries. While nothing is an absolute guarantee against war, logic suggests that trade dampens the inclination toward it. Since trade, in most cases, suffers in war, it follows that the financial interest of those who are engaged in trade is strongly tied to maintaining peace. Countries act on interests; as countries are, in many respects, the sum of their citizens, the more citizens they have who hold a personal interest against war, the less they are inclined toward it. At the least, a country engaged in trade is less inclined toward war than it would be if it had no trade and thus no citizens with a personal financial interest against war.[133] Furthermore, trade relations serve often as the starting point for international organizations which tend to greater peace and prosperity: recall that the European Union began as the European Coal and Steel Community.

Trade deficits, moreover, are a smokescreen conjured up by protectionists.[134] If the United States has a trade deficit with Mexico, that is because it has surpluses elsewhere, or is generating enough domestic wealth or credit to purchase imports; Mexican merchants are not giving away their wares for free. If a country has trade deficits, it is because it can afford them; they are, in a way, a sign of economic strength, provided proper maintenance is given to the national debt.

Having thus labored to describe the general nature and benefit of trade, we shall now turn to the present situation of these United States and answer the arguments for protectionism. When Hamilton called for tariffs, he recognized the benefit of free trade, but pleaded that circumstance forced the young Union to disregard it: the new Republic inhabited a mercantilist world, and had not the influence to make the states of Europe desist from their own protectionist policies.[135] Had our Republic opened itself to trade then, it would not have been reciprocated; the gain it would have realized by freely importing European manufactures was, in Hamilton's reckoning, of lesser value than that obtained from building U.S. manufacturing capacity, which a tariff could hasten.[136]

Half a century later, Great Britain caused those circumstances to change. Britain in 1846 was the mightiest economic power; it could bear the inconvenience of being the first to eliminate its tariffs and thereby enable all to reap the benefits and follow its lead. This is to say, free trade needs a great power as its champion: it benefits all, but only if the world is conducive to it, and only the largest economies have the clout to make that so. The United States in 1791 could not have been that champion. Fifty years later, Britain could, and was; and a century thereafter, our Republic finally took the torch from the fading British Empire, and in so doing compelled the latter to dismantle the imperial preference tariffs that it had devised during the Great Depression.

Our Republic, despite its recent retreat from the arena,

remains in a position to be free trade's champion today. But be warned: if it should persist in laying down that role, China will pick it up. As the economic mass of that country has grown, its gravity has drawn the lanes of world commerce slowly toward itself and away from these United States.[137] If our Union, in its fit of ill-temper, should continue to forfeit the advantages of trade while China and the other nations of the world continue to enjoy them, this drift shall accelerate and become irreversible. To reject free trade is therefore to cede wealth, influence, and leadership to a rival power; any American patriot, however concerned he or she is about jobs, ought to take pause at that thought.

As for jobs, although shifts in trade may at times displace them, protectionism shall not regain them. Supply and demand alone govern the production of goods and thus the creation of jobs. The decades after the Second World War brought an ample supply of manufacturing jobs because world demand for American manufactures was high; but that demand was fated to fall as other countries rebuilt their factories from the wreckage of war. Yet the instinctive response to this inevitable decrease in world demand – to adopt tariffs – shall only cause it to diminish further, as other countries retaliate in kind. A few jobs added to meet the domestic demand for certain manufactures, as a result of a tariff, shall not compensate for jobs eliminated by the loss of demand abroad for other products; nor shall it outweigh the increase in the cost of living that accompanies a fall in trade.[138] Demand cannot be restored by protectionism; it may, however, be restored by competition.

Competition, we concluded in our previous essay, compels firms to provide quality goods and services at affordable prices; and this logic applies as much to the market outside the United States as it does to the market within them. Indeed, American firms, when they must compete with foreign ones, can and shall produce excellent goods and sell them at attractive prices. By so doing, they shall find those goods to be in demand across the world. This in turn shall cause them to invest and grow; and the growth of those firms shall increase the supply of jobs.

Protectionism, by contrast, extinguishes competition. It allows inefficient firms to linger in business far longer than they naturally ought to, preventing their workers from learning skills that are relevant to new and competitive industries. As domestic firms dither in this way, those new industries are instead mastered by foreign companies; then, once the protected firms become so inefficient that even tariffs cannot save them, their workers are sent tumbling onto the racetrack to start anew after they are already several laps behind. Trade protection, moreover, allows domestic monopolies to hide from foreign competition, thus freeing them to raise prices, depress wages, and prevent new entries into the market.[139] Free trade breaks this stranglehold; and insofar as competition from abroad prevents monopolies from manipulating the cost of goods at home, it may thereby open a door for new domestic firms to enter industries that use such goods as input.

Our critics shall point out, however, that it matters little to American workers that their firms are competitive if those firms outsource to foreigners the jobs generated thereby. We first note that this charge is often exaggerated: firms that grow as a result of free trade may outsource some jobs created by that growth, but it is rare that they outsource all of them; and even a single job thus created at home is one more job than would have existed without trade, and of benefit to the citizen who attains it.[140] Firms that nevertheless rely excessively on outsourcing, if they exist in a competitive market, shall sooner or later be undercut by foreign firms that are local to the country on which the outsourcing firm depends.

American firms which are wise, therefore, shall make the most of American talent; and it is incumbent on those firms and on American workers themselves, with some assistance from their government at all levels, to cultivate that talent. For jobs cannot be stolen, but they can be won or lost; and for the workers of this Republic to find suitable and sustained employment, they must make themselves competitive in the world market. We have full confidence they can do so, as did Hamilton.[141] We do not desire to shield our fellow citizens from the rigors of the world, but to prepare them to go forth and meet them. We thus offer several proposals to reopen world trade to free competition, to assist the American worker in becoming competitive, and to prepare him or her for the shocks and displacements that inevitably accompany shifts in trade.

First, the Trans-Pacific Partnership ought to be restored, with full U.S. participation; obnoxious measures added to the re-negotiated North American Free Trade Agreement ought to be removed;[142] the Trans-Atlantic Partnership ought to be negotiated to a swift conclusion and ratified by the Senate; and a free trade agreement ought to be negotiated with Britain upon the finalization of its exit from the European Union. These actions, taken together, shall substantially restore and enhance the world system of free trade, with our Republic at its center.

Not only do trade agreements bring prosperity to our Union:

by improving economic relationships, they grant it influence abroad. The abandonment of the Trans-Pacific Partnership shamefully ceded initiative to China in a region that is vital not only to the United States' wealth, but to their security, for the countries of East Asia guard the approaches to Hawaii and the West Coast.[143] Restoration of that agreement is thus vital to the upkeep of U.S. power. The countries of Europe, by virtue of their position on the western sea lanes leading to our Republic, and those of North America, by their location along our Union's land borders, warrant similar regard. As for Britain, the special relationship between that country and ours, which was christened by Roosevelt and Churchill but hearkens to a common history, ought not to be discarded lightly; the United Kingdom, adrift from Europe, ought to find a safe harbor with these United States.

Second, our Union, in concert with those countries which ascribe to the principle of free markets, ought to challenge China and other countries that profess support for trade abroad while interfering in the market at home. State capitalism is not true capitalism, and it distorts free trade by denying fair competition: China closes its market to foreign firms or extorts secrets from them before granting entry, yet it gives state funds to its own firms to gain them market share abroad.

Yet to challenge unfair competition by revoking free trade is to fight fire with fire, which merely burns everyone. Better to fight fire with water: rather than erect broad tariffs to choke off trade with China, which hurts producers in these United States, our Republic ought to target, with conditional measures, those firms that are owned or funded by the Chinese state in contempt of the market until Beijing shall reform them.[144] Moreover, it is better to fight an inferno with a fire brigade than to attempt its extinguishment with a single hose. Our Republic therefore ought to cease its present trade disputes with Europe and Japan, whose own firms compete fairly, and enlist their aid in challenging China's standing in the World Trade Organization.

Third, state governments should encourage private provision of unemployment insurance plans by investing a portion of the initial capital necessary to put those plans into operation. That shifts in supply and demand, occurring rapidly across the entire world, will periodically cause American workers to lose employment is a reality that must not be ignored. Rather than despair of this eventuality, citizens of this Republic ought to plan for it, just as they do for the possibility of a car accident, by paying into an insurance plan when they are gainfully employed, and then receiving a payout from it if they are displaced from their job. If properly insured in this way, citizens will be assured of valuable time with which to recover, retrain, and re-enter the arena. They shall know, too, that rather than being rendered dependent on the charity of others during their period of hardship, they instead draw from funds that they themselves prepared beforehand: they, and no other, continue to provide for their families even as they search for new work.

Fourth, state and local governments, whenever possible in partnership with private firms, ought to fund courses for re-training and skill certification in public colleges and universities, so that their workers can react rapidly to shifts in global demand and compete in new industries.[145] Public institutions of higher learning, as we argued in our previous essay, are worthwhile objects for investment by the States. They ought, however, to expand their offerings beyond four-year degrees, so as to be of greater service to a greater number of people; one way to do so is to offer short-term courses which bestow formal certification of a skill that is useful to industry. Special emphasis ought to be given to robotics, given the extent to which automation has caused the dwindling of industrial jobs. Those whose previous functions have passed to computers might, if properly trained, return to the arena as the operators and maintainers of those very machines.

Fifth, Congress ought to pass legislation to guide the development of artificial intelligence, so that robotic systems do not one day render human workers redundant. Whereas trade may displace jobs, automation has the potential to eliminate them altogether. Yet such an outcome is not predestined. We seek laws crafted on the principle that every machine, no matter its artificial intelligence, ought to be supervised in some way by a person; and this principle has not only an economic component, but a moral one, which we shall discuss in a later essay.

Sixth, governments at all levels ought to remove barriers that obstruct the re-employment of workers in new industries. This object may be achieved in part by reducing license requirements to the minimum level necessary to prevent harm to consumers, and, in industries where rigorous licensing is in fact necessary, by simplifying the procedures through which new workers earn their license. Doing so shall make it easier for a citizen who is experienced in one industry affected by a shift in trade to apply his or her skill to another industry that is growing.[146]

Seventh, temporary anti-dumping measures still ought to be imposed selectively on goods produced in excess of demand by foreign state-owned or subsidized enterprises, so as to prevent a sudden crash in a domestic industry. Government-sponsored enterprises can afford to sacrifice profitability in order to attain monopolistic market share; and while such lopsided competition may be free, it is not fair. The temporary nature of anti-dumping measures is vital, however: they are meant to balance supply and demand, not to restrict trade, but if left in place indefinitely they become a tariff. Their intended end is not to shield an uncompetitive industry, but to let an otherwise competitive one weather a brief foreign surplus, or instead to allow an uncompetitive industry to die gradually rather than suddenly, so that the transfer of its workers to a new field can proceed in an orderly and effective manner.[147]

Finally, as with any general principle, that in support of free trade must admit of a few exceptions. The first, and most obvious, is that our Republic must preserve industries critical to its national defense.[148] It must retain both the institutional knowledge and industrial capability to procure military hardware and provisions, such as fuel, either domestically or by importation from allies which are close both politically and geographically.[149] The second, with Hamilton's reasoning in mind, is when our Union is in need of developing some new industry which is both clearly defined and essential to the future security or prosperity of these United States. This latter condition has not lately been present on a wide scale, because American firms are already in the lead of new industries, mainly technological, that contain promise for the future.

The last regards foreign ownership of American firms or means of production. Although such ownership generally does no harm, and can be beneficial so long as the owning foreign firm pays U.S. tax for its operations in our Republic, it becomes a matter of concern if the object intended for takeover is essential for the national defense, as aforementioned, or if such acquisitions reach a point wherein the majority of industry within a U.S. State is managed by foreigners. In such a circumstance, accountability would be lacking between American workers, their employers, and their government. Such a scenario is unlikely; due to the ingenious and competitive nature of American firms and workers, past, present, and future, our Republic faces no shortage of national heavyweights in the realm of international commerce.

Thus, fellow citizens, is free trade a necessary component of free enterprise; and the competition it engenders around the world, if properly structured to ensure fair play, can offer far greater prosperity than the illusory refuge of protectionism. The people of these United States are raised on competition, and we who are Americans today ought not to shy away from it.

No. 9 – On Citizenship

That citizens are the building blocks of a republic – That these United States must grow but they ought no longer to conquer – That extending representation to territories is the only just and lasting means of ruling them – That Puerto Rico ought to become a State – That the other territories and the District of Columbia ought to have voting representation in the House of Representatives – That the House of Representatives ought to be enlarged – That the Census ought to be carefully protected from interference and well provided for – That American Indian nations ought to have oversight of federal agencies that manage their distinct interests – That public authorities ought to give priority to protecting the right to vote – That the law ought to be upheld evenly – That our Union has long had an Anglo-Hispanic character

> "I am glad to see one real American here." —Robert E. Lee, greeting Ely Parker, a military aide to Ulysses Grant and a Seneca Indian, at Appomattox.

> "We are all Americans." **—Parker's reply to Lee, April 9th, 1865.**

NO. 9 – ON CITIZENSHIP

In our previous few essays, we addressed matters of economics, by which a republic is maintained; in the following two, we focus our attention on citizenship, by which it is built. It is by the consent of its citizens that a republic is created and by their industry that it grows. They provide its power, its creativity, and its character; they are bound by oath to protect and preserve it. Those republics which have a great number of committed citizens are the mightiest countries; those which neglect or disenfranchise a part of their citizenry, or spurn opportunities to gain new citizens, are fundamentally weak.[150] To preserve both its enlightened character and its unparalleled might, our Republic must strive to retain the sincere affection of its citizens and to increase their number. The former may be achieved by representation in government and equality before the law, and the latter in three ways: new births, territorial expansion, and immigration.

The birth of new generations of Americans is always welcome, and it may be encouraged by government, yet it may not with any justice be compelled.[151] We shall address immigration in our next essay. Here we shall reflect upon our Union's past acquisition of territory, and consider matters related to the consolidation of that acquisition through just and equitable citizenship.

That there have been severe injustices in regard to these matters in the history of the United States cannot be denied. Yet it is also evident that our Republic has striven to right its past wrongs, and in so striving it has made a moral progress, gradual but firm, that marks it out in the history of the world. Nonetheless, some failings still remain. In the overseas territories, some joined to our Union for a century or more, reside four million citizens who lack true federal representation, yet they have for decades been paid little attention by the residents of the fifty States. Within the boundaries of the continental United States, citizens who reside in the District of Columbia are not represented in Congress; tribal nations, though their individual members are accorded full representation as citizens of the United States, often hold little sway as a body politic over matters that affect their distinct interests; and rights already guaranteed by law to all the citizens of our Republic, which include the fundamental right to vote and the right to receive due process of law, are in various ways infringed upon.

We propose to correct these discrepancies; to ensure full political representation to all citizens, as is their right; and in so completing the process of Union, to secure to our Republic the full blessings of liberty and the might bestowed by the wholehearted devotion of its citizens,[152] and to belie those who assert that ours is not a just and enlightened nation.

All things of mankind are in motion; they expand or contract, rise or fall.[153] This maxim is particularly true for large countries, as Rome once was and these United States are now; and expansion, either in wealth, population, or territory, leads to a country's rise, whereas contraction brings about its fall. When Rome ceased to grow, it began to decline; the United States ought to strive to avoid this fate. Yet whereas Rome was founded in bygone times and, in accordance with bygone principle, grew itself by conquest, our Republic was born in the Age of Enlightenment and matured into an appreciation of those principles which its founding proclaimed; and among them is that a conqueror has no moral right to rule indefinitely those whom he has conquered by force of arms, no matter how just his cause.[154] Not long ago, our Union respected this principle: it vanquished Germany and Japan in just war, but then returned their government to their people.

It may appear that we have created a paradox: that these United States must expand, but ought no longer to conquer; and, moreover, our Union holds territory today which in the past it gained by conquest. Yet the history of Rome offers a clue to resolving this contradiction, and the history of our own Republic offers the solution.

Rome, unique in its time, held its conquests by extending its citizenship to the inhabitants of the lands it conquered. As they came to enjoy the same rights as the residents of Rome itself, they, too, worked to maintain its empire; it is no surprise, therefore, that the glory of Rome long endured while that of other olden states soon dimmed. Centuries later, when the British Empire strived to equal that of Rome, the American States rebelled against it; and they revolted against Britain not because of some unbridgeable chasm between the two peoples, for then there was little difference between them, but because they were denied representation in Parliament. It was for similar cause that the rest of the British Empire departed in the centuries to follow:[155] Britain established government over them by conquest, which bestowed no enduring moral right to rule, and sustained it without full citizenship and representation, thus never establishing such a right.[156]

The thirteen States first remedied that injustice by governing their Union in a Continental Congress, which represented each State as a body politic. They then established a Constitution to represent both the States, in the Senate, and the people directly, in the House of Representatives. The Constitution was imperfect in its early years, as our Republic expanded across the continent: some of its people were held unjustly in slavery, while others were denied citizenship or the right to vote. Successive generations forged a more perfect Union: by constitutional amendments and wise acts of legislation, they extended full rights of citizenship to all those born or naturalized on U.S. soil. Thus, whereas our Republic began its expansion in North America with conquest, it followed with citizenship and representation, which in time included all those whom it once had conquered.[157] Such representation permits the Union to govern justly all fifty States today.[158]

Yet mainland Americans tend to forget that four million of their fellow citizens reside in five overseas territories that have shared the history and experience of these United States for a century, yet are to this day excluded from full membership in the Union. Their representatives in Congress have no vote; their delegates cannot influence Presidential elections by casting votes in the Electoral College; and, as is now shown in Puerto Rico, such lack of influence frustrates their ability to recover from hardships. Yet they pay U.S. tax, contribute recruits to the U.S. military, and are governed by U.S. law.[159] They were first brought under U.S. jurisdiction by conquest or purchase, which itself bestowed no lasting moral right to rule, and their present status is one of taxation without representation, which all Americans know sustains no such right. This condition ought not to be continued indefinitely; rather, full representation ought to be extended to them.

Furthermore, the District of Columbia, which was established by the Constitution as the seat of the federal government and was never meant to become a State, now contains over half a million permanent residents – more, indeed, than Wyoming, the smallest State. Our Republic's Founders withheld statehood for that district for the reason that no State ought to exert undue influence over the government of the Union by holding sovereignty over the grounds where that government convenes. This logic remains valid today. Yet to deny the district's citizens any vote in Congress is nonetheless unjust. Any city, even one built for the sole purpose of convening a government, must have permanent inhabitants in order to function: for if no one lived there to work in its restaurants or shops, federal officials would have no food to eat, nor any place to buy essential goods. People must live in the District of Columbia; those people are citizens of the United States; and all citizens of the United States ought to be represented in Congress.

The American Indian and Alaska Native tribes, over five hundred in number, dispersed widely across the territory of the Republic, and counting on their rolls nearly three million of its citizens, have long been considered under U.S. law to be 'domestic dependent nations,' and as such have direct ties to both the federal and state governments.[160] A full description of their legal station is beyond our scope, but a few characteristics are abundantly clear: they, like the several States, enjoy a measure of partial sovereignty; tribal members are, by virtue of unequaled history of residence in America and clear establishment in U.S. law, citizens of the United States;[161] and, as citizens, they hold the indisputable right to vote and be represented in government.[162]

Today, two and a half centuries after our Republic's founding, those rights are finally, in large measure, respected by the government of the United States. Yet the Indian nations' exercise of the partial sovereignty due to them by solemn treaty, over the matters which constitute their distinctive interests, is often hindered on account of those nations' dispersal across the continent and their unique position within the several States. Representation in the management of those affairs ought, as a matter of right and also of sound policy, to be accorded them as a body politic.

We therefore offer several proposals to ensure full representation for all citizens of these United States, and in so doing to achieve a more perfect Union. We undertake to accomplish this aim without undermining the principles and institutions that buttress our Republic, such as the partial sovereignty of the States and their equal representation in the Senate. We seek not revolution, but reform. We, citizens, must remain faithful to the enlightened logic of our Union's founding; we must recognize that the wrongs of past times, and their enduring legacy today, are a blighted exception to such high principles; and our efforts to redress the sins of our forebears must refine our Republic according to its original design, rather than demolish it.

To that end: Puerto Rico ought, with the consent of its citizens, to be admitted as a State after the 2020 Census of the United States. It is entirely qualified for statehood on account of its size: its population, as estimated presently, is more than three million, twice that of Hawaii. The present economic hardship of that territory ought not to obstruct its admission to the Union, for the fundamental logic in favor of statehood – that all citizens of this Republic ought to have representation in the federal government – is political rather than economic.

Nor ought Congress or the territorial government to dither on statehood with halfhearted referendums, designed to create deadlock by the inclusion of several ambiguous options and tied to no immediate action. While obtaining the consent of

Puerto Rico's citizens is, in our view, indispensable to just rule, the lawful power of conferring statehood rests with Congress; so, too, does responsibility for bringing the matter to decision. Congress ought without delay to pass an Act that shall establish Puerto Rico as State upon its ratification by a territory-wide vote, as it did for Alaska and Hawaii, thereby presenting our fellow citizens with a free, fair, and clear choice.

The other inhabited territories – Guam, American Samoa, the Northern Mariana Islands, and the U.S. Virgin Islands – are geographically dispersed and, at present, each has a population smaller than that of many mainland cities; the largest, Guam, is less than a third the size of Wyoming, whose own population is merely an eightieth of California's. A nod must therefore be made to practicality: were those commonwealths each to be represented separately in the House of Representatives, that body, in order to maintain proper proportion for existing States, would have to swell to an unmanageable size.[163] To combine them as a single State, however, would be a manifest injustice: their circumstances are too varied to be provided for equitably by one state government. Yet if statehood is not the answer, principle nonetheless demands that the citizens resident there be granted representation in Congress and the Electoral College.

We therefore propose that, by means of constitutional amendment, Congress grant those territories a voting delegation in the House of Representatives, akin to the method that was used by the States in the Continental Congress. Under such an arrangement, the four territories would together form a delegation, whose composition is in proportion to their respective populations; and that delegation would have one vote in the House, as the smallest States do.[164] The delegation would decide, by an internal vote of its members, which way it shall cast its Congressional vote for each act of legislation. We further propose that those territories together be granted Electoral College votes by extending to them the 23rd Amendment, which today provides electoral votes to the District of Columbia in proportion to its population but not exceeding that of the smallest State.[165] The territories may then choose to divide between themselves the three electoral votes they would receive under such an arrangement, as Nebraska and Maine do with their districts.[166]

Combined representation of the above type is a practical matter made necessary by small populations and geographical dispersion; in contrast to combined statehood, it would allow each commonwealth to continue governing its own affairs while gaining a say in the Union. Should the number of permanent residents in any one of those territories someday increase so as to make viable the prospect of statehood, Congress ought then to offer it without delay.

The District of Columbia, in accordance with the logic of the Founders, also ought not to be made a State; but that logic does not go so far as to assert that its residents ought not to have representation in Congress. The influence of a partly-sovereign local government in the federal capital was the matter of concern. On that premise, it is reasonable that the district's government not hold the representation in the Senate that is the preserve of the States; but it is not reasonable that its people be denied representation in the House. We propose that the district be given voting seats in the House of Representatives in proportion to its population, which exceeds that of the two smallest States. Its present formula for Electoral College representation, explained above, ought to remain the same, for the reason that the Electoral College is meant to represent both the people directly and the States; it is thus appropriate that the District of Columbia's residents are represented therein, but that the city as a body politic may not outweigh the votes of States.

Should these proposals become law, our Union would consist of fifty-one States and two special representative districts, the U.S. Overseas Commonwealths and the District of Columbia. Astute readers, however, will note that the present ratio of seats in the House of Representatives to the populations of the several States is itself flawed: Montana has nearly twice the population of Wyoming, for instance, yet has the same number of representatives. One of our Republic's most prominent newspapers recently proposed that chamber's enlargement, noting that the discrepancy was caused by legislation which, without clear constitutional necessity, limited the size of the House to 435 members.[167] We concur that a flaw exists and that it undermines the purpose of the House of Representatives; we propose that it be resolved by legislation after the 2020 Census, concurrent with the extensions of representation proposed above.

Moreover, determining, as it does, the allocation of seats in the House of Representatives, the Census is fundamental to the working of our Republic; it thus ought to be shielded vigorously from interested tampering and carried out with the greatest possible precision. We call, therefore, for the Census Bureau to be equipped with the most useful modern technology and funded in keeping with the vital role that our Union's Founders accorded it.

In regard to the American Indian and Alaska Native nations, we propose the formation of a representative body, composed of those nations' delegates, which shall advise the three federal agencies charged with fulfilling our Union's treaty obligations to them – the Bureau of Indian Affairs, the Bureau of Indian Education, and the Indian Health Service – and exercise some authority over the expenditure of funds which Congress appropriates to those departments. That those agencies manage affairs that affect tribal nations' distinct interests, as stipulated by treaty and separate from the interests of the whole public, is clearly evident; it is appropriate, therefore, that those nations, as partly-sovereign bodies politic, should have some oversight of them. In this way can those bureaus depart fully from their past existence as the forlorn receptacles of broken promises and become more accountable to those whom they are meant to serve.

On that matter, we must also comment on the means that have been used, in the past and in recent times, to obstruct tribal members and other citizens from exercising their fundamental right to vote. Of late, controversy has risen around requirements, instituted by state governments, for presenting identification to vote or register to vote. We consider it reasonable for citizens to identify themselves before they vote, but the means for doing so must freely be available to all; and when there is conflict in that regard, public authorities ought to give priority to protecting the right to vote, without the free exercise of which there can be no Republic.[168]

It may also be said, proudly, that the moral triumphs of our Republic are reflected in its laws, and none more so than the first section of the 14th Amendment, which enshrines a single, equal citizenship for all people born or naturalized in these United States.[169] Since the ratification of that Amendment, many worthy laws have been passed by Congress and the States that reinforce the promise of liberty contained within it; yet since that time, and to the present day, those laws have not uniformly been upheld. In a republic, the law is and must always be the highest source of authority; and if it is upheld only selectively, the foundations of the republic shall weaken and crumble.[170] We thus urge vigilance from all citizens and from governments at all levels, so that laws may be applied with constancy and fairness; and to ensure such an outcome, it is necessary that those entrusted with applying the law are never placed above it.

We conclude with one parting note relating to Puerto Rican statehood. It has been much remarked that Puerto Rico, were to it be admitted to our Union as a State, would be the first State to have a Spanish-speaking majority; and there are some who worry that its Hispanic culture is out of step with the national character of the Republic. To this apprehension, we counter that the United States has had a partial Hispanic character since the admission as States of Texas and Florida in 1845. Our Union had before then been largely British in its common culture, owing to its descent from the British Empire; but by admitting those two States and the six others which for centuries were part of the Spanish Empire,[171] our Republic made itself heir to both the British and the Spanish legacies in North America and became, in a way, itself a part of Latin America. In a similar way is our Union the successor to the storied legacy of the French in North America and to the American Indian empires and confederations, whose names echo across its history and landscape and whose descendants form a part of our Republic's might today.

Rather than fear Latin influence, therefore, citizens of these

United States ought to recall that it has long been present, and embrace our Union's Anglo-Hispanic character. Our Republic ought then to use this aspect of its heritage to full advantage in its diplomacy with the countries of Latin America, much as it used its British roots to forge lasting and mutually advantageous ties with Britain, Canada, Australia, and New Zealand. Yet before we turn to the subject of diplomacy, we must complete that of citizenship, by addressing in our next essay the challenges and opportunities of immigration.

No. 10 – On Immigration

That being American is civic, not ethnic – That all peoples can be made into U.S. citizens – That expanding lawful immigration is beneficial to the Republic – That the Union's borders must be secure – That entry ought to be lawful and orderly – That birthright citizenship is inviolable – That the unlawful immigrants now present in these United States ought to be made eligible for citizenship upon payment of a restitution – That immigrants ought either to seek U.S. citizenship or eventually return to their home country – That dual citizenship ought to be discouraged – That those seeking citizenship ought still to be required to learn English – That citizenship ought to be expedited for immigrants who are willing to settle in an area which has economic need for them

"I hereby declare, on oath, that I absolutely and entirely renounce and abjure all allegiance and fidelity to any foreign prince, potentate, state, or sovereignty, of whom or which I have heretofore been a subject or citizen; that I will support and defend the Constitution and laws of the United States of America against all enemies, foreign and domestic; that I will bear true faith and allegiance to the same; that I will bear arms on behalf of the

United States when required by the law; that I will perform noncombatant service in the Armed Forces of the United States when required by the law; that I will perform work of national importance under civilian direction when required by the law; and that I take this obligation freely, without any mental reservation or purpose of evasion; so help me God."
—U.S. Naturalization Oath.

In our previous essay, we wrote of how our Republic might secure the affection of all its citizens by completing the unfinished work of Union. In this one, we address one of the foremost means by which these United States gain new citizens: the immigration of people from around the world and their naturalization here. Immigration is bound inextricably to citizenship; the one cannot be comprehended without the other. Yet public debate has lately regarded those topics in isolation. It has become fashionable either to decry immigration as the cause of all ills and slam shut the gates to it, or instead to declare unconditional love for all newcomers in such haste as to demand no attendant obligation from them. Both approaches discredit the principles, history, and traditions of these United States. Our Republic ought to welcome those who in earnest desire to make it their home, but it ought also to require from them the full responsibilities of citizenship.

Citizens, we recall, are a source of strength for a republic: they fight in its armies, pay its taxes, create and labor in its commercial enterprises, and uphold its reputation abroad. As a greater number of people can, if well employed, do a greater volume of work, it is a matter of simple logic that the more citizens there are who owe allegiance to a republic, the mightier that country becomes.[172] Immigration brings in people from beyond our Republic's borders; assimilation and naturalization make them into devoted citizens, who give the same pledge to support and defend the Constitution as do members of the armed forces. It is largely in this way that our Union has attained its present stature. Absent contrary evidence, it ought then to be supposed that the same means shall continue to augment these United States' prosperity and might.

Some opponents of immigration, in search of such evidence, assert that certain peoples, on the basis of their prior nationality, are not suitable to become U.S. citizens. To this, we say that there is no ethnic character to being an American; there is only a civic one.[173] Nor has it been any other way since the Republic's founding, or else by the logic of blood and soil none but the American Indian would have the right to citizenship here.[174] If the Founders had thought their loyalty due to their ethnic kin, they would have had no grounds to revolt against Great Britain: most were Englishmen or Scots, and Britain is home to Scots and Englishmen. Moreover, also present at the founding were a great many black Americans, some of whom as free men joined the battle for independence; and others, though they were held unjustly in bondage, nonetheless toiled and fought to build this Republic, and so had the right, if not yet the title, to citizenship.[175] Our Union, indeed, was born amid diversity.

In its infancy, our Republic needed to grow so as to stand equal to the powers of Europe. To this end, it opened its doors, and through them came Irishmen, Germans, Italians, Poles, and more.[176] Many of those new citizens spilled their blood for our Union in the great wars of those times; their effort and industry, together with the labor of those born on U.S. soil, forged our Republic into the mightiest country in the world. Any citizen who bears an Irish, German, Italian, or Polish name thus ought to reflect upon this history before asserting that a Mexican, an Arab, or a Korean has nothing to contribute to these United States; to do so would deny not only his or her ancestors' legacy, but also the Republic's founding principle that all men are created equal.

To that, our critics may retort that all people are created equal, but all societies are not. It is true that some societies inculcate their members with beliefs that run counter to our founding principles; and this occurrence must be taken seriously, for a republic based on a civic identity can be eroded if the principles underpinning it are disregarded by its citizens. But we contend that all who in earnest desire to leave those societies and take the obligation of citizenship in the United States, our Republic can mold into good citizens. Furthermore, while immigrants of the first generation will often hold, consciously or not, onto the customs of their home country, their children, raised within our Union, will almost without exception consider themselves first and foremost to be American and instinctively hold dear the founding principles of the Republic.

It may, however, be noted that the ability of a country to assimilate immigrants depends on their number. Yet the present quantity of immigrants to the United States cannot be presumed to degrade this ability. Our Union today has a population of three-hundred and thirty million; ten thousand refugees from Syria, or even a hundred thousand from Central America, are thus mere raindrops in the ocean. For our

NO. 10 – ON IMMIGRATION

Republic's character to be distorted by immigration, a majority would have to be formed by new arrivals before they could assimilate. Such a shift has little danger of occurring. At present, our Union admits between seven and eight hundred thousand immigrants a year, roughly equivalent to a quarter of one percent of the whole population. Were that number to be multiplied by four, so as to be just over three million or one percent of the population, it would even then take a century for immigrants arriving after 2019 to outnumber everyone here today; and by that time, the first of them – or rather, their descendants – would be as well-assimilated as our fellow citizens whose ancestors came to these United States in 1919.

It could instead be claimed that even if all immigrants become exemplary citizens, our Union has no capacity for them. Yet this is a weak assertion, for our Republic is a vast country which still holds wide expanses of sparsely populated land, and whose largest cities pale in size to the metropolises of Asia. Nor, as is sometimes claimed, does immigration bring financial hardship. All countries at times face recession, whether they admit immigrants or not; its causes are usually such things as paucity of credit, overburdening regulation, or rampant speculation, which are errors made by those already resident. Indeed, the arrival of new people, if well-regulated, adds both to the demand for goods and to the capacity for producing them, and thereby grows the economy. Moreover, though in certain circumstances a large increase in immigration might prompt a small decrease in wages, any diminishment in pay ought to be attended by a drop in the price of goods, which are produced more cheaply as a result of cheaper labor. If it is not, that is the fault of monopolies, which stifle competition, not of immigrants, who invigorate it.

We note also that, just as the differences between the States give our Union an advantage over its rivals, so too does the diversity of backgrounds among Americans. It multiplies our skills and talents, makes our foes familiar – for we have brought to our side their former citizens – and builds on that great American strength in war, observed with much consternation by our enemies, of being unfamiliar and unpredictable to rivals who themselves are monochrome and doctrinaire.

All this we have said in favor of immigration. But we assert also that, for those not born or naturalized in these United States, residency in this Republic is a privilege, not a right; and if immigration is not well regulated, it will be a source of discord that strains our Union. The torch of Rome shone brightly while that empire made citizens of all races and origins, but it faded when Rome admitted whole tribes into the empire's borders without making them Roman. For our Union to long endure, its citizens must have common principles and a common purpose; it may thus be multicultural only to the extent that its new citizens can adapt their old customs and forms of organization to the principles of liberty and the purpose of preserving the Republic.[177]

Moreover, as there are costs related to the reception and settlement of immigrants, and because a rapid increase in population can cause economic disruption, there must be attendant laws to ensure that immigration occurs in an orderly manner. To flout these laws is to disregard the sovereign will of these United States, to deny tax revenue to our Union's governments at all levels, and to do an injustice to those immigrants who obeyed the law of their adopted country and thereby bore the inconvenience of migrating lawfully. Unlawful immigration is therefore a trespass and nothing but; circumstances may mitigate it, but not negate it.[178]

For those born on the sovereign territory of these United States, however, citizenship is an inviolable right. That certain legislators and officers, at the apex of our government, do now question that right is a fearful step on the dim road to illiberal democracy. Those officers claim that they merely desire not to reward those who cross the Union's borders illegally with the hope of giving birth on its soil; and it is true that such acts are obnoxious, insofar as they from time to time occur. Yet the consequences of revoking the birthright are twofold and sinister.

First, it creates a forsaken class that holds no right of citizenship anywhere. A child, born in the United States to unlawful immigrants, might not be guaranteed citizenship by the country of its parents. That child did not come into being there, but here; that country thus has no more obligation to the child than this Republic has to the parents. Such children would grow and live without citizenship in either country, and their children would suffer the same fate. As citizenship is the foundation of civic rights, every generation born this way would be condemned to abuse. To punish the child for the trespass of the parent is directly contrary to the enlightened character and principles of our Union, whose Founders recognized such an act as shameful long before the 14th Amendment enshrined into law the right to citizenship at birth.[179]

Second, should the 14th Amendment be subjected to arbitrary interpretation,[180] before long it shall be interpreted so as to exclude from citizenship any persons whom a particular party or officer in government might find objectionable. To accept such action would be to submit to the basest form of tyranny. We shall say no more on the matter, save that the citizens of these United States, which once declared independence from foreign tyranny, ought never to accept tyranny at home; and thus they ought to uphold the right to citizenship at birth on the soil of this Republic, which is and shall always remain free soil.

Having thus established our principles, we now offer several proposals for consideration by the public. First, the current quotas for legal immigration ought to be modestly expanded, and thereafter maintained at a ratio of the whole population, rather than set at a fixed number. We do not presume here to determine the particular quantity – for that is the duty of Congress, after a period of due debate – but, for the sake of illustration, we suggest that annual issuance of legal permanent resident visas, which today stands at seven hundred thousand, or less than a quarter of one percent of the whole population, be increased to a third of one percent, which in numerical terms relative to the present population would amount to slightly over one million.[181]

We further propose that the largest portion of this increase be allocated for employment-based immigration, which at present constitutes but a fifth of permanent residency visas issued.[182] We do so because our argument for an expansion of lawful immigration is not one of generosity or pity, nor purely philosophical, but rather one of national interest. These United States coexist in the 21st century with several other great powers, all of which send many of their promising citizens to our Union to be educated. It is absurd and self-defeating that our Republic provides to these individuals its excellent education, only to evict those of them who desire to remain.

The 'brain drain,' as the wish of the well-educated to emigrate to America is known, is a boon to our Republic.[183] It is made all the more so by the ability of Americans to assimilate those talented arrivals, make them good citizens, and allow them to prosper in our free market and thereby contribute to the common wealth. If we deny them this opportunity, we forfeit our gain. Moreover, if we, for instance, send a promising Chinese student whom we have educated back home against his will, he shall thereafter harbor a feeling of bitterness towards the United States, which before he admired; and by doing so we shall have compounded our error, in that we not only forfeited his talent, but returned him to a rival nation which may use his skill against us.

In the case of less-educated immigrants, the hard logic of interest still applies. A greater number of people, as we noted above, can do a greater amount of work, whether that work be menial or exalted. The great powers of this century include the giants of China and India, whose multitudes far outnumber the population of these United States; and as they develop in efficiency and modernity, in time their economies shall dwarf our Union's, unless it narrows the imbalance by continuing to grow.[184] Our Republic's workforce cannot compete by bringing in doctors alone, and therefore we propose that new permanent residency visas be allocated to both skilled and unskilled workers who show merit in relation to their means of livelihood.

Second, any expansion of lawful immigration must be accompanied by sustained efforts to patrol and secure the inhabited and accessible sections of the borders of the United

States,[185] and to enforce immigration laws. The United States, as any sovereign country, has the right to guard its borders and, at times, to close them, and has the obligation to enforce its laws. To suggest otherwise would be to invite anarchy. Thus, we call for vigorous policing of known routes across the Union's borders so as to prevent unlawful migration, smuggling, and other crimes.

Furthermore, for the purpose of managing sudden surges in attempted migration in a just and lawful manner, we propose an expansion of judicial capacity for matters of asylum and deportation. Our Union, as we noted in previous essays, is in need of more judges; and this is especially so for cases related to immigration, which require timely resolution.

Third, unlawful immigrants already present in these United States, so long as they have committed no crimes,[186] ought to be permitted to earn citizenship upon payment of a restitution. As they have violated the law by their manner of entry into this Republic, it is logical that they ought to make amends in some way before they may be admitted to the body politic as citizens; and as unlawful entry imposes costs on the public, it is fitting that this penance be financial. This restitution could take the form of a personal tax, paid over a period of time, both to the federal government and to the government of the State in which the person resides. Until payment is complete, moreover, the person concerned ought not to be eligible to receive public welfare or pension. Such benefits are a privilege bestowed by the body politic upon its members, and as such ought not to be disbursed to those who are in debt to it until that debt has been cleared.

In this regard, also, the principle of not punishing the child for the trespass of the parent ought to be observed: for those who immigrated unlawfully to these United States as children, the restitution ought to be reduced or exempted. Furthermore, lest our proposed policy engender a belief that trespassing the Union's borders is permissible so long as the trespasser can pay the penalty for doing so, it must be entirely clear that this proposal is a practical matter which applies only to the unlawful immigrants living on U.S. soil today, and is not meant to be repeated.

Fourth, all immigrants seeking U.S. citizenship ought to be required to learn the English language, as is the case today. A civic nation, as we mentioned above, can only persevere if its citizens adhere to the principles and institutions that underpin it, which are themselves derived from the history and culture of the country. The most enduring and accessible source available to the immigrant for learning the values, traditions, and legends which comprise this civic culture is his or her fellow Americans – those present, with whom the immigrant may converse, and those past, whose original works the immigrant may read.[187] To tap this source, a common language is necessary; in our Union, that common language is and has been English.

In practical terms, furthermore, new citizens who can associate on neighborly terms with their fellow Americans shall, on the whole, be better informed of their surroundings, have access to more opportunities, and lead a more satisfied and fulfilled existence than those who, by virtue of not sharing in the common language, remain isolated from the majority in their adopted country. Indeed, English, in addition to being the common language of these United States, is at present the foremost language for commerce and exchange around the world. Its instruction may thus distinctly be considered a public good and an indispensable part of public education.

Fifth, citizenship ought to be expedited for immigrants who choose to reside in locations outside of existing immigrant clusters, if the local government requests their settlement. There are, across these United States, localities which have declined or stagnated in population, or which suffer a shortage of labor or of certain professions necessary for the public good; and these cities, towns, and counties might determine that the arrival of new residents is very much in their interest. Yet they are often far from the immigrant's imagination, which is usually fixed on New York or Los Angeles, or other large cities where a multitude of recent immigrants already reside. We thus propose that the federal government, by consulting the several States, keep an annual list of municipalities whose local authorities have requested the settlement of new immigrants, and that immigrants be informed of these locations on receiving their permanent residence visas; and if they settle in one of those places and can prove their residence there, they ought then to be compelled to wait only three years before becoming eligible for citizenship, rather than five.

Such a policy has a threefold advantage. It aids the diversion of new immigrants to areas where their economic contribution shall be greatest, thus building prosperity for those localities and for the Union; it hastens the assimilation of immigrants by drawing them away from large clusters that allow new arrivals to fall back on their home country's language and habits; and it gives citizens, through their local governments, some say in the settlement of newcomers, so that they may mitigate their apprehensions and instead seize immigration as an opportunity.

Sixth, foreign citizens residing in our Republic, who do

not represent their government or firm in a diplomatic or commercial capacity, ought, after a certain length of residence, to be required either to seek United States citizenship or else return to their home country. No country ought to be expected to give an indefinite right of residence to an individual who does not both contribute to the commonwealth and owe it undivided political loyalty. It is well and good that legal permanent residents pay tax to the Union and their State of residence; but only the oath of citizenship obligates them to come to the Republic's defense if required by law and charges them with the right and responsibility of participating in its governance. Such a commitment is what distinguished the Roman citizen from the person who merely lived in Rome's empire, and it is still this spirit which animates great nations today. Thus, after ample time is given to reflect and prepare, the question of citizenship ought to be put before all foreign residents, either to accept without reservation and become truly American, or to decline and amicably part ways.

Seventh, dual citizenship ought to be discouraged, except for countries closely allied with these United States whose association with our Republic binds them to its defense.[188] While it is logical for a citizen to owe allegiance to different levels of government – local, state, and federal – when all are under a common head, it is contradictory for a person to owe allegiance to two independent, sovereign entities not bound by treaty. If a treaty exists but is broken, dual citizenship ought to end with it, for then there is no guarantee that the interests of our Union and those of the other country will not come into conflict; and no country can resolve a conflict to its advantage if it cannot be assured of the allegiance of its citizens.[189]

In the case of children whose circumstances render dual

citizenship necessary, they ought to be recognized as such until reaching adulthood, at which point they ought then to decide with which nation their first allegiance lies. As for individuals whose families span two countries, and who today hold dual citizenship as a means of facilitating travel between them, we propose that, should they choose to renounce their U.S. citizenship in favor of the other country, our Republic instead grant them a visa which enables them to travel to and visit within these United States with relative ease. Our Union ought then to urge other nations to reciprocate, so as to provide for the access of those who choose to renounce their citizenship abroad in favor of the United States. This, we reason, shall satisfy compassion by allowing close and continuing contact between kin, and thereby encourage individuals to opt for one, undivided citizenship.

All that we therefore advocate for immigration, we do for the sake of obtaining citizens who are staunchly committed to our Republic's well-being and mindful of their duties to it. We welcome immigrants to these United States; we do so with the full expectation that their political commitment to our Republic shall be singular, and that they leave behind, in accordance with their citizenship oath, any loyalty to foreign governments they may once have held; and we desire that they build their new lives in this land shoulder-to-shoulder with their fellow Americans, and in so doing ensure that our Union ends the 21st century as strongly and proudly as it ended the 20th.

No. 11 – On Foreign Policy

That building might is necessary for maintaining liberty – That preserving the preeminence of republican forms of government is the highest foreign policy interest of the United States – That allies which advance this high interest ought to be held dear – That allies which advance a lower interest should be favored only while that shared interest persists – That our Republic ought to confront foes only so long as they threaten U.S. interests – That limited uses of force can support diplomacy – That diplomacy ought to continue while force is used – That China is the principal rival of the United States in this century – That our Union is a maritime power – That the Pacific Ocean is the main arena for our Republic's contest with China, but not the only one – That our Union ought to strengthen relations with other maritime nations – That the U.S. military ought to re-emphasize training and the upkeep of equipment – That lesser challengers distract the United States from its main effort – That moral imperatives sometimes alter the rules of the Great Game

"Speak softly and carry a big stick; you will go far."
—Theodore Roosevelt, January 26th, 1900.

In our previous two essays, we discussed how the United States may secure to itself the full blessings of its vast territory and growing population, which together comprise a great part of our Union's might. Might, we say, is the combined weight of population, resources, and territory, plus the political and administrative organization that enables a country to bring its weight to bear on matters affecting its interests.[190] Competent governance, which we examined earlier in this series, accumulates might. Here, we shall focus on the use of might: that is, on foreign policy, which is the conduct of the United States – herein, a singular Union – toward foreign governments in the perpetual contest of nations to secure their interests. This competition was once aptly described as a Great Game, and our Republic's goals in it ought to be to maintain the peace and to uphold the preeminence of the United States and its allies, by which free government may be preserved.[191]

All countries strive to protect their population, resources, and territory and to ensure that they are able to procure the items they require from abroad. Republics, being accountable to their citizens, have an additional consideration to satisfy: they must maintain their freedom, for their people's lives and property are never secure if left to the depredation of a tyrant. Thus, the first duty of the United States is to its people, and the first object of that duty is to preserve the liberty that the citizens of our Republic enjoy.

That much is evident. Yet the logic which proceeds from it, in regard to events abroad, is not as readily apparent. Citizens of republics, content with the freedom they enjoy at home and desiring to avoid the trouble of the world, invariably ask why enlightened countries cannot be content to be pacifistic, prosperous, and inward-looking. Our answer is that the choice of peace or war will not always be left to them, but may be forced upon them by the aggression of another; thence the only way to preserve their liberty is to possess the might to defeat or deter the aggressor.[192]

Some citizens, acknowledging this truth, might argue that a republic ought to fight when necessary to defend itself, but should otherwise pay little heed to the outside world. Yet since the might of future aggressors cannot be known, a republic must have the capacity to grow its own might to meet the threat that may someday face it.[193] This requires the republic to draw resources from beyond its borders and to find allies abroad. Great Britain, had it remained Little England and not acquired its empire, could not have stood alone against Nazi Germany; without allying with the United States and Russia, it could not have vanquished that foe. Our Republic, had it not expanded across North America and made alliances around the world, could not have overcome the Soviet Union, which had itself spread across Asia and installed vassals throughout the globe.[194]

The creeds of pacifism and isolationism are thus not merely self-destructive, but morally flawed. Decency in government must be accompanied by might, or else a republic will sooner or later be defeated, and its decency left to the mercy of an aggressor who has none; and might can only effectively be built and preserved by looking abroad. Republics must play the Great Game.

The first principle of that contest is that interests, not relationships, are paramount.[195] This wise maxim, when steadfastly adhered to, ensures that the well-being of the Union is not subject to the personal relations between its leaders and heads of state abroad, which ebb and flow with the fleeting impulses of personality and affection rather than the hard dictates of national interest. Yet, if interpreted in a superficial manner, it may be abused to justify discarding reliable allies in favor of momentary friends. A wholesome examination of this principle is therefore in order.

The paramount interest of our Republic is to preserve its liberty, which is best done by maintaining enlightened government as the dominant force in the world. A nation benefits from the presence of others that are governed in its image: their inner workings are better understood by it, and so it can sooner reach accord with them. That is why Athens aligned with other Greek democracies; it is why the fascist states in Germany, Italy, and Japan banded together in the past century; it is why Russia once spread communism and now seeks to spread illiberal democracy; and it is why China extols the alleged virtues of unvarnished autocracy. It follows that our Union ought to strengthen other countries that practice republican government, for they, by their nature, share the interest of preserving it; and it ought to be wary of those that embrace dictatorship, for they, by their nature, oppose that interest. It is natural that most of the countries friendly to the United States today are republican in nature, whereas those most averse to it are dictatorial.[196]

Old republican allies thus remain so because their systems of government advance this institutional interest, which supersedes narrower considerations. Allies of this type may diverge from our Union on occasion, such as when France objected to the invasion of Iraq, yet remain firm friends. But if they shed their republican institutions and degenerate into tyranny, their worth as allies shall extend only so far and so long as they serve a lesser purpose. Such was the case during the Cold War of several third-world tyrants, whom the United States aided principally to contain the menacing spread of Soviet might and afterwards upbraided for their despotism.

There are therefore two classes of ally: one that shares institutional interests and another that shares narrow interests. Relations with the former ought to be of longer duration and greater closeness, and allowance ought to be made in them for differences in policy; whereas the latter ought to be given greater scrutiny and less tolerance for divergence.

The same principle applies to foes. Those which plot to undermine or overpower free government menace our Republic's institutional interest and ought to be dealt with sternly; but if they cease to do so, they ought no longer to be considered beyond the pale. Yet even the most hostile and subversive states are rarely irreconcilable in all affairs. If a temporary arrangement with them serves U.S. interests, then our Union ought to make one, for a refusal to negotiate rarely accomplishes anything for either party.[197] Lesser foes, moreover, ought to be treated as opponents only so long as they threaten narrow interests. If the conflict of interest ends, with it should end all resentment held by the government and people of the United States towards that country.

Thus may relations be brought in line with interests. If an alliance no longer supports any institutional nor narrow interest, it ought without hesitation to be ended; if rapprochement with an erstwhile foe serves an institutional or a narrow interest, and if an accord on the latter does not prejudice the former, it ought to be struck without regard to present sentiment or past insult.

The second principle of the Great Game is that all national

means must be used in concert to advance national interests. The tools of foreign policy are understood to consist of negotiation and force, the latter of which may include both military and economic coercion. All of these methods are and ought to be closely intertwined, and they are not limited to conventional modes of war and diplomacy. Russia has understood this truth clearly: its use of 'hybrid warfare,' in which it employs in tandem propaganda, foreign aid, diplomacy, sanctions, proxy war, special operations, and conventional arms, has in recent years won Moscow both territory and influence.

The United States, by contrast, has fallen into the habit of placing too much and too rigid distinction between force and negotiation, such that it either loses influence through reluctance to act, as it did recently in Syria, or overreacts when moved to fight, as it did before in Iraq. Yet our Union was once able to exercise all aspects of its power in such a mutually-reinforcing way, and can again;[198] and it can do so in a more humane manner, and in support of a more decent end, than does Russia. But it must first remember how, and here we shall offer a few thoughts.

Clausewitz is often cited for his maxim that war is but politics by other means.[199] It may be derived from this thought that all war is politics, though not all politics is war. It follows that the United States ought not to take up arms without a political aim, nor use them with the sole intent to destroy its foe – which is costly and impractical – but rather to advance its interests. It must also keep in mind that its opponents have political considerations of their own. By taking astute note of them, our Union can settle conflicts more to its advantage and in a lasting manner.

Our Union must therefore conduct diplomacy while waging war; it must talk continually as it fights. That does not mean it must be friendly to adversaries whose acts are repugnant, only that it must communicate with them; and if they are willing to make concessions that satisfy its interests, it should allow them to back down with dignity. A foe that saves face among its own allies and citizens is less likely to return to the fight, for it shall have less political compulsion to do so than it would were it humiliated by the stronger power.[200] If our Republic adheres to this practice, it will find that its battles are in general less bloody and of shorter duration, and more likely to succeed; for having first thought through what it intends to achieve, and limiting itself to that object, it shall be less apt to fall into the excess zeal or aimless drift that ruin armies.

Challenges to our Union's interests, moreover, ought to be met with alacrity and vigor when they first arise, lest they grow to such proportions that they require a general conflict to resolve. Indeed, a general war between great powers is to be avoided at most costs, because such wars are so destructive as to harm severely the interests of all sides: recall the First World War, which ruined two empires – Turkey and Austria – crippled two more – France and Britain – and sowed the seeds of vicious tyranny in Germany and Russia. The best way to prevent such war is not by pacifism or appeasement, but for it to be made clear in advance which side would win in battle and which encroachments would cause that country to fight.[201] Small uses of force, or even mere threats of force, so long as they are made with a mind to politics, can show capability and resolve and thus bring the necessary clarity to those vital considerations.

Yet the use or threat of force serves no useful end if it is accompanied with belligerence and unpredictability, and may instead cause grave harm. Bellicosity is provocative, but adds no substance to might; unpredictability blurs the line beyond which a country is prepared to embark upon a general war. Either trait invites escalation that negates the purpose of early and vigorous action, which is to resolve a conflict in favor of our Union's interest.[202] To resort to a large use of force to settle a dispute that could have been solved by a small one, or by a mere demonstration, is to act against that interest, for the blood and treasure of our Republic's citizens would then have been expended without need.

Credibility, therefore, ought to be prized: our Republic ought to state what it is prepared to do and, when necessary, to do it.[203] By conducting its affairs in such a way, it may be assured – as much as is possible in the affairs of mankind – that it will only use force when force is needed, and only in such proportion as necessary. For if an opponent proceeds with its challenge in the face of a credible threat, then either it is testing this credibility, in which case it shall refrain from further encroachment once the promised response has been given, or else it has resolved to try its fortunes in battle, in which case battle is inevitable.[204]

Yet as harmful as it is for a country to act without stating its intention, so is it disastrous for a country to state its intention but then not act. Inaction often results from fear of escalation; yet it generally encourages escalation on the part of the adversary, who realizes he may obtain that which he desires by acting aggressively. The damage to a nation's interests in such an event, moreover, is not limited to the conflict in which it occurred nor to the countries involved in it. Reputation cannot be fled from, and credibility cannot be kept if it is not continually maintained. Every move our Republic makes in the Great Game is observed by all of the contenders therein; every success is noted by them, and every stumble registered.[205]

By considering force as but one tool, therefore, to be used in tandem with negotiation and all other aspects of power, the United States shall find itself less inclined either to shy away from confrontation or to be carried away by it. Our Union has spectacular and singular might; if used in a way that is sensible, credible, and forceful, it will advance U.S. interests and keep the peace.

We shall now depart from the realm of maxims to survey the Great Game in this century. Today, our Union still stands preeminent; it is also the mightiest republican power and therefore the natural champion of free government in the world; no other champion has emerged, as the United States did upon the decline of Britain; and thus our Republic may not cede its position as first among the great powers, or it will have allowed liberty to take second place to tyranny.

There must be no mistaking that China is the foremost of those rivals which challenge the dominance of the United States and its republican allies, and that China is assisted in this regard by Russia.[206] Our Republic must, however, strive to maintain its preeminence without resort to general war with either power, as the struggles of the past century could not equal the destruction wrought by total war in the nuclear age. Yet, to achieve this feat, it is necessary that our Union maintain the might to prevail in any war, whether of limited or general scale, and the credibility to convince its challengers that it has the will to do so; and it must possess these qualities without bombast, which could push a rival to fight who otherwise would yield. Our Republic must heed Theodore Roosevelt's advice: it must speak softly and carry a big stick.

Furthermore, our Union must bear in mind the particular characteristics of its geography. It spans a vast continent, from which it can draw abundant resources, but is separated by two oceans from the more populous hemisphere. Its prosperity relies on freedom of navigation, and its security on command of the high seas.[207] The United States is thus fundamentally a maritime power, though one which is capable of amassing military strength on land when circumstance demands it. It declared this truth when Theodore Roosevelt sent the Great White Fleet around the world; proved it in the Second World War, when our Union gained dominion of the Atlantic and Pacific while fielding a large army in Europe; and demonstrated it again in the past decade, when sorties from our Republic's aircraft carriers battered the 'Islamic State' in distant Iraq and Syria.

China, by contrast, is in certain respects a mirror image of our Union. Though similar in territorial extent, latitude, and climate, it rests on an edge of the great landmass of Asia and so looks for its prosperity and security not only to the Pacific and Indian Oceans, but also to the overland routes that have for millennia bound it to the populous regions of the Middle East and Europe. China is thus fundamentally a land power, but one which is capable of building military strength at sea when circumstance allows it – and it is presently doing so.

The Great Game in this century shall therefore come to a contest between two powers which are in some aspects alike and in others opposite: both vast, both industrious, both able to project power on land and at sea; but the one a republic, the other a dictatorship, and each reliant on somewhat different avenues of trade. The outcome shall turn, we believe, on the great issue of which power becomes the world's economic center,[208] and on which power exerts greater control over that avenue of commerce which is vital to them both, the Pacific Ocean.

To hold its own in this contest, the United States must wisely build and wield its national might. We shall here divide might into three types: economic, diplomatic, and military. It is an artificial division, for each relies on the other and in a successful policy they function as a whole, but it can usefully illustrate some our Republic's priorities in the 21st century's Great Game.

Economic might we define simply as the wealth of the Republic and its citizens, which is acquired by growing the national economy through efficient utilization of our Union's resources. It is naturally of core importance to the object of maintaining the United States at the world's economic center. Accumulated wealth also enables our Republic to purchase essential goods, to raise and maintain armies and fleets, and to hold influence abroad through trading relationships, among myriad other benefits. We shall not dwell on it here, because in several previous essays we examined at length how our Union may prosper through competition, free trade, and prudent management of public debt. We shall note only that the United States ought to be sparing in the coercive use of its economic might. Tariffs, embargoes, and sanctions, if employed excessively, have a twofold danger: they encourage other countries to craft new economic arrangements that avoid our Union, and by stunting one part of the world economy they might reduce growth in other, unforeseen parts of it and thus diminish our Republic's own prosperity.

Diplomatic might, which is commonly known as influence, we define as our Union's ability to access resources and places that are important to its interests and to deny those things to its foes. It is acquired chiefly through negotiations with foreign governments. Among the benefits that can be derived from it are overseas bases, rights of transit across foreign territory, the sharing of information, agreements for the supply of important materials, and allied military support.

The United States, as a sea power that depends on oceangoing trade, ought to reinforce its influence across the maritime edges of the world: Latin America, Western Europe, the coast of Africa, the Indian Subcontinent, Australia, Southeast Asia, Korea, and Japan. The Republic of India, which rivals China in size and promise but has embraced free government, is of singular importance in this regard; and there are other nascent republics, possessing large populations and future potential, such as Nigeria, Indonesia, and Brazil, that the United States would be wise to invest in good relations with.[209] Our Union is aided in this endeavor by the fact that several of the countries in these areas emerged, as our Republic did, from the British and Spanish Empires, and so have similarities in language and culture to the United States; and even the nations that do not share those legacies often have kinship bonds between their citizens and Americans who once emigrated from their shores.

Furthermore, it is sound strategy in any contest for a contender to dominate wherever he has the natural advantage and to mount a challenge wherever his foe's natural advantage is most tenuous; this way, he forces his foe to labor to maintain his position rather than being forced by his foe to maintain his own. So, too, is it in the diplomatic aspect of the Great

Game. The United States must view the maintenance of its influence in the above-mentioned maritime regions – where it has the natural advantage – as an imperative to be tended to at all times; but it ought also, when opportunity arises, to contest Chinese influence in the land areas of the Middle East and Eastern Europe, which connect China by land to the West. By virtue of the potential for Chinese trade along that route, Beijing has a natural advantage there: recognizing this, China has already begun to augment its influence under the auspices of its Belt and Road Initiative.

Moreover, as the western Pacific and, to a lesser extent, the Indian Ocean are the areas in which the advantage of our Republic relative to China is the most tenuous, our Union must expect China to vigorously contest U.S. influence there, as it has done in the South China Sea. The United States ought to meet these challenges with equal vigor, and understand that they are not isolated instances, but part of a grand strategy meant to diminish our Union's diplomatic might.[210]

Military might, the last of our three divisions, consists of the strength and competence of our Republic's armed forces, which is accumulated principally by training soldiers and procuring equipment. It is measured by the ability of those forces to triumph once battle has been hazarded; and if known to be considerable, it deters foes from attempting the use of force at all. Our Union has in the past few decades attained a reputation for formidable military might, and it is indeed well-earned, but no country can rest on its laurels for long. China is now developing formidable sea power even as it maintains the largest land army in the world, whereas Russia has modernized its own forces. Our Union's military authorities recognize the need to meet these developments;[211] its citizens ought to enable them to do so, and expect them to do so wisely.

Maintaining military might requires that our Union preserve its qualitative advantage, for it cannot exceed China in its number of soldiers nor Russia in its willingness to sacrifice them. The superiority of American arms is ascribed to high technology, and rightly so, but this focus is misleading when directed to narrow projects that are expensive, excessively complex, uncertain, and time-consuming.[212] Rather, the U.S. military ought to invest in technologies that have wide and versatile uses, as it did with the refinement of military radar in the Second World War and the development of satellite positioning in recent times. All new technologies are uncertain, but versatile ones are likelier to pay off in some way, even if their ultimate benefit is unforeseen.

Broader effort ought also to be devoted to training,[213] supply, and the replenishment of existing equipment which is known to be reliable. Particular attention in this last respect ought to be paid to the ships of the U.S. Navy; unlike armies, fleets cannot quickly be raised, as it takes far longer to build a ship than it does to train a soldier or assemble a tank. The National Guard ought also to be expanded, so as to enable our Union to swiftly mobilize if circumstances so require. By thus revitalizing the time-honored American tradition of the militia, moreover, the United States can increase the forces at its disposal in a way that reinforces the relevance of the several States and reduces somewhat the present gulf between soldier and civilian in American society.

There remain aspects of might that do not fit neatly into the categories we have defined here. Notable among these are the ability of the United States to inspire ordinary people abroad, known as 'soft power;'[214] to invent and master new technologies; and to maintain an adequate supply of strategic resources. Our Republic may preserve the first by conducting its own affairs in keeping with its enlightened principles. It may see to the second by means of an open, competitive, and vigorous economy; we shall propose certain ethical bounds for invention in a later essay. The third requires foresight and planning, and here we have two notes: that the late revolution in energy production through 'fracking' has been a boon to our Union by freeing it from reliance on foreign gas and oil and by keeping low the world price of those commodities, and talk of banning it is thus self-destructive at this juncture; and that our Republic ought to take further measures to ensure its access to rare earth minerals, which are necessary for production of computer chips and at present are almost entirely obtained from China.[215]

As we approach the end of this essay, we have so far offered thoughts on how our Union can maintain its position relative to its principal rivals. There are, however, lesser challengers that divert U.S. might and distract our Republic from preserving its primacy among the great powers. The most pressing among these are jihadist groups, North Korea, and Iran: the first must be vanquished, and the others contained until they cease their hostility to the United States.

Jihadist groups, having as they do an irreconcilable ideology and an interest in turmoil, do not fall entirely within the principles of the Great Game outlined in the first part of this essay; they must be dealt with unconditionally in some ways but carefully in others, lest our Republic exhaust itself in pursuing them. This is not to say that extended operations against them ought never to be undertaken; at times, as in Afghanistan after 2001, those have been necessary. But such campaigns ought to be avoided if possible, for they sap blood and treasure and leave U.S. forces exposed to rivals who would send proxies against them. When those battles must be fought, our Union ought to fight them through its own local allies, as it did to defeat the 'Islamic State' in Iraq and Syria.[216] North Korea and Iran, by contrast, ought to be treated in accordance with the ordinary principles of foreign policy. Those maxims do not deny the use of force when force may be useful, but any force used ought to be limited and support the aim of containment.

The Great Game is a contest of extraordinary complexity, and we could muse about it without end; but this essay must end if it is to be read, and it is not at any rate meant to provide detailed strategy. We have but one final point to make. Several of the arguments we have made herein are based upon cold calculations of interest and might; and that is well and good, for in normal times it is best to play the Great Game dispassionately. The interests of China would, in many instances, conflict with those of our Republic even if China were not ruled despotically, and it is well to remember that the people of China do not pursue those interests out of villainy or hatred, but because they, too, seek security and prosperity for their country.

Yet there are times when moral imperatives enter into the contest of nations, and the rules of the Great Game must yield to them. Our Republic has encountered such instances in living memory, when totalitarian states attempted to expand across the world and it became the duty of all enlightened nations to fight them. The short-lived 'Islamic State' was one such menace, and the United States did its duty to defeat it, though the cost to us was small. The Soviet Union was also such a threat at points throughout its sordid history, but, by good fortune and shrewd strategy, our Union prevailed without fighting it directly. So, too, were Nazi Germany and Imperial Japan, which our Republic vanquished in a struggle that spanned the world – yet it did so with confidence that it would have greater prosperity after victory. We do not make such qualifications to degrade what our Republic has achieved in those moments, because its achievements have been great. We do so only to show that the decisions to fight were made easier by a reasonable certainty of success.

The ultimate moral test of nations is to face the choice to fight in defense of fundamental and decent principles when the result is uncertain and ordinary maxims of foreign policy urge against it; that is, to choose between shameful surrender or, at best, the prospect of Pyrrhic victory.

Britain faced such a test in the Second World War. After the defeat of France in 1940, it had the opportunity to make peace with Germany, for Adolf Hitler's ambitions lay primarily to the east. Conventional wisdom demanded that Britain reach such an ignoble arrangement and thereby avoid a general war that it was then ill-prepared to fight. It is to the eternal credit of the British that they refused to do so, and stood alone for that fateful year, knowing full well that prolonged war would likely end in bankruptcy, if not invasion and occupation by one of the most ruthless tyrants known to history.[217] Countries, even enlightened ones, often accumulate much moral ambiguity throughout their histories, and such was certainly the case with the British Empire; but on its day of reckoning, Great Britain proved itself beyond doubt to be both decent and brave.

Our Republic made such a choice once, too. In 1860, it stood on the brink of disunion, facing the prospect of a terrible civil war, threatened by a class of men whose fortunes depended on the unimpeded expansion of slavery. Had our Union consented to shield that evil institution then and forever, it might have avoided the cataclysm to come; and doing so might well have seemed the rational move in the view of foreign policy, for a nation divided against itself is weakened in regard to its foreign rivals.[218] But the United States rejected that dark temptation, persevered through its hour of trial, and so imprinted its enlightened legacy firmly onto the pages of history.[219]

Thus, fellow citizens, we urge you to uphold our Republic's legacy. The United States must have an eye to its place in the world; it must build its might and wield it wisely; and it must summon the will, as it has before, to do what is right even in difficult times. In this way shall our Union be remembered not merely as a passing contestant in the Great Game of nations, but as a great nation, like Rome and Britain before it, whose deeds and courage advanced the progress of mankind. It is to this latter subject that we shall turn in our remaining two essays.

No. 12 – On International Cooperation

That some great works are beyond the ability of one country alone – That a reform of international institutions is needed for those works – That international cooperation requires some constraints on sovereignty – That sovereignty may not be limited without some form of political association between countries – That confederation is a useful form of association for dynamic collaboration – That international institutions ought to be purposeful, potent, and representative – That some institutions ought to offer varying levels of commitment – That equitable contributions are best secured by weighted voting – That contributions can be in kind – That the United States ought more readily to form international institutions with friendly republics than with autocratic rivals

> "What is at stake is more than one small country; it is a big idea; a new world order, where diverse nations are drawn together in common cause to achieve the universal aspirations of mankind…" —**George H. W. Bush, State of the Union address to Congress, Jan. 29th, 1991.**

In our previous essay, we put forth ideas for how our Republic may preserve and wield its national might. Yet even while the United States of America remains the greatest of the world powers – as we insist that it be throughout the century ahead – there are nonetheless some great works that neither our Union nor any other nation can accomplish alone in their entirety, but must instead achieve in cooperation with the other countries of the world. Among these tasks are the control and eradication of diseases, the maintenance of the world economy, the establishment of technological standards, the conservation of our Earth's wildlands, the halting of global warming, and the exploration of outer space. We shall examine some of these tasks themselves in our next essay; here, we shall focus on the international institutions that may be used to accomplish them.

International cooperation is ingrained into the history of our own Union, which came into being, in many respects, as an alliance and trade union of thirteen sovereign States. In the 20th century, our Republic turned again to formal associations between countries, this time spanning the globe, to address the world's challenges and extend its own influence. For seven decades, that system of institutions, including such names as the United Nations, the World Bank, the International Monetary Fund, NATO, and the World Trade Organization, kept the general peace, rebuilt the world economy, and withstood the threat of communism. It came to be known first as the free world, and then, in time, as a world order led by the United States.

Yet the world is always in motion, and no system that remains static can endure forever.[220] So it has come that the present world order is under strain from those, both within

NO. 12 – ON INTERNATIONAL COOPERATION

our Union and abroad, who now question its purpose, potency, and representative nature. That order has indeed reached a limit, and it must be reformed and reinvigorated so as to advance the interests of our Republic and other enlightened societies throughout the 21st century. We thus call for a reform of the American-led world order that recasts international institutions honestly as confederations, carefully bounded in scope and accountable to their member nations yet possessing the means to achieve their ends. To succeed in this endeavor is to prolong the Pax Americana for another century or more, and so reap the peace and prosperity that it bestows; to fail is to see that era reduced to a wistful memory, a bygone triumph whose vast promise was squandered by neglect.

The first and greatest question regarding cooperation between independent nations is that of sovereignty. Sovereignty is the exercise by a body politic of its general will; it cannot be given up without dissolving the political community from which it stems, although it can be limited by transferring power or by promising or forswearing certain acts.[221] In a republic, the general will is expressed through the vote of representatives elected by the people, and sovereignty may not be limited without their consent. As any collaboration with a foreign country necessarily places some constraint on sovereignty – because each government must, at minimum, refrain from acts that would impede the ability of the two countries to work together – it follows that in a republic any binding terms of foreign collaboration must be approved by the legislature. For this reason, our Republic's Constitution requires the Senate to ratify treaties, which thus become U.S. law.[222]

That manner of reconciling international cooperation with

the general will is well suited to short projects or fixed accords whose fulfillment requires little discretion. Such compacts were common at our Union's founding.[223] Yet it is ill fitted to the collaborations prevalent today, which are generally of longer duration and dynamic in their execution. Modern technological advancements have both enabled and rendered imperative such close and extended cooperation between countries, for events in one nation now rapidly affect the entire world. Yet any such collaboration, though it may be agreed upon in general terms through a ratified treaty, requires decisions to be made in response to particular developments on the ground; and any decision so made risks adding a new constraint to sovereignty.[224]

Thus, it becomes necessary to establish a more responsive form of association between countries so as to enable the people of each to consent to particular decisions made in the pursuit of a common enterprise. We ought, then, to review the ways in which this end can be achieved. There exist four forms of political association that govern cooperation between peoples, which differ in the degree to which they limit the sovereignty of their constituent parts. Some of them are well-suited for domestic governance, others for international collaboration.

The first form is alliance, which we define here as any league, be it military, commercial, or otherwise, wherein the contracting parties transfer no power and limit their sovereignty only to the extent that they each agree to carry out or refrain from certain acts. No governing body is established to mediate between them or to enforce terms. Although the parties may consult from time to time, their governments are the only medium through which popular consent is conveyed,

NO. 12 – ON INTERNATIONAL COOPERATION

and decisions are made by consensus between them. Alliances are as old as mankind, yet their faithful fulfillment has been the exception rather than the rule.[225] This is due to the fact that they are rigid and have nothing to bind them but the mutual interest of their contracting parties. Because considerations of interest change, the time soon arrives when one party's interest no longer wholly aligns with the others'; because there are no means of modifying the terms of the alliance except its renegotiation by all parties, often the recourse of the dissenting party is to threaten to withdraw. The alliance is put to the test; usually it fails. Alliances that survive the longest are generally those that are tested the least,[226] but if their terms are so seldom applied, then the cooperation they are meant to achieve is practically meaningless.

The second form, on the other extreme, is unitary government. There, all power is vested in a central government, which exerts authority upon individual citizens directly. Though it may grant autonomy to subordinate entities within its jurisdiction, it bears no obligation to do so and may withdraw such autonomy at will. Unitary government functions best for the governance of small republics: most U.S. States, internally, have this form of government, as do many small countries abroad. When applied to large populations and territories, however, it tends to neglect the varied interests contained therein and degenerate instead into a tyranny of the majority, which then becomes a tyranny of one.[227] We have argued vigorously throughout this series against the application of this form of association to the United States, and it follows that we soundly reject its application to the world. All attempts to bind the world tightly under a single government have begun as base tyranny and failed in

163

bloodshed; and it shall always be so.

The third form is federation, in which the constituent parts and a central governing body each limit their sovereignty by dividing power between themselves, with each retaining a partial share. Certain powers are granted to the center, whereas others are reserved to the various parts. The constituent parts do not possess the right to leave the federation; representation is given both to the people directly and to their partly-sovereign bodies politic; and the federal center exerts its enumerated powers upon individual citizens directly.[228] This form, of course, is that used by the United States, as well as such other countries as Germany and India; and, as we have reasoned throughout this series, it is the best form for governing large republics, insofar as a federation can both act vigorously and maintain liberty. Yet the political will to establish federations between countries does not exist today, nor is it likely to absent an overwhelming and immediate interest: to join a federation requires countries to substantially constrain their sovereignty, which they are loath to do so long as conditions allow for a secure, independent existence.

The fourth form is confederation, which also apportions power between a governing body and its constituent parts, but favors the parts. The central body has fewer powers allocated to it; it exercises its powers through the governments of its parts, not on individual citizens directly; and each part reserves the right to withdraw from the confederation. Confederation is inadequate for governing a republic, as the experience of the United States has shown.[229] Yet, if well designed, it may be effectual for international cooperation: unlike alliances, confederations can adapt to the times and penalize recalcitrance; unlike unitary governments or federations, they do not require their members to substantially constrain their sovereignty. This is especially so if a confederation is limited to specific ends and does not presume a general responsibility for its members' affairs.

Alliances were the most common form of cooperation before the world wars; but when the alliance system failed manifestly to prevent the deaths of tens of millions in those struggles, the leaders of our Republic and of other countries turned to institutions to govern the interactions between them. Many of these institutions were founded upon treaties, but are confederations in key aspects: the United Nations, the European Union, the International Monetary Fund, NATO, the World Bank, and others all have permanent governing bodies that assume some powers, however small, from their member countries; all exercise those powers through their member governments, not on citizens directly; and all allow voluntary withdrawal from their ranks.

Confederations they are, but some have long been flawed in their design. The experience of world war at first hid those shortcomings: the desire to avoid another catastrophic conflict caused many countries to work in concert regardless of the failings of the institutions created for that purpose. Then the Cold War came, and those flaws could be explained as a consequence of the confrontation between East and West. When the Soviet Union fell and the United States rose triumphant, our Republic's might again masked the deficiencies of this world order, because countries would cooperate with its institutions to avoid crossing our Union. But now the world wars have faded from memory, new rivals have filled the void left in 1991, and the Iraq War has revealed a limit to American might, and so the flaws of the prevailing world order stand bare.

That some existing institutions are deficient is made evident by recent developments. The United Nations could not deter Russian aggression against Georgia and Ukraine, nor end bloody repression and war in Syria, nor effectually rebuke North Korea's acquisition of nuclear arms; the European Union lost Britain and could not prevent Poland's and Hungary's slides into illiberal democracy; the World Trade Organization can only look on as trade groans under the weight of tariffs thinly justified under exceptions to its own rules. Three shortcomings make this so: international institutions, though noble in intent, often lack purpose, power, or representation.

When an institution lacks purpose, it achieves little, for it does not know what it wishes to achieve. Such is the case for several regional associations whose bland pronouncements, while regularly issued, are all soon forgotten. As international institutions are not general governments, their purposes cannot be assumed: they must be stated explicitly within the institution's founding documents. Moreover, the more focused the purpose, the more effective the institution shall be. The International Monetary Fund possesses this quality, insofar as its purpose is known to all and can be expressed simply: it exists to make loans to countries that are at risk of default. Its entire structure is designed to support this function; as a result, it fulfills its purpose on a regular basis, earning, at turns, both praise and opprobrium, but never finding itself ignored.

Others, such as the United Nations, possess a discernible purpose, but lack altogether the power to achieve it.[230] This result arises because the means necessary to an institution's ends have not been allocated to it in its founding treaty, or because the mechanisms of exercising them have been designed so as to render their actual use impossible. It is true that confederations always have difficulty in compelling their constituent parts to take actions contrary to their parochial interest. This disadvantage, however, may be mitigated in two ways. The first is to establish the purposes of an institution in proportion to the common interest that may be expected from its members. To create an institution, for instance, which includes Saudi Arabia and Iran, and to set as its purpose the provision of security would be folly; but to set as its purpose the maintenance of a high price for oil invites success.[231] The second is to establish a means for the governing body to penalize recalcitrance in one area by denying benefits in another:[232] for instance, the European Union can withhold common funds from member countries that violate its regulations.

The European Union, in turn, has both notable ends and the ability to attain them, but has brought upon itself such popular resentment that its very continuance has from time to time been threatened. The complaint has been of insufficient representation in its governance.[233] Just as the principle of non-delegation, which we examined in our essay on bureaucracy, forbids elected legislators from delegating their lawmaking power to unelected agencies at home, so too does it forbid delegating that power to unrepresentative institutions abroad. The violation of this principle is the gravest danger to a confederation: the resentment it sows ensures that, if not reformed, the confederation will either dissolve or become despotic. It is thus necessary that the governing body of an international institution neither take on a life of its own nor be captured by a minority of its members, but rather be held continually accountable to the whole.

We thus posit that all international institutions ought to have clearly defined and carefully limited ends, power to achieve those ends, and a vigorous representative system to make rules necessary and proper to the institution's purpose, and that these traits be codified in a founding treaty. If this standard seems similar to most enlightened forms of government, that is because it is: systems of governance between countries, which all international institutions are to a degree, ought to mirror just systems of governance within countries, but with their ends limited to those objects which the joining nations determine is worth limiting some of their sovereignty to attain.

A model approaching this ideal is the European Space Agency. Its purpose, to explore the reaches of outer space and conduct civil research therein, is limited and clear; it possesses its own funds and personnel, and is working to develop its own facilities, all of which give it power to achieve its ends;[234] and at regular intervals it convenes a representative council of its members to determine its budget and objectives, thereby rendering it accountable to the countries it serves. It has in this way enjoyed several decades of quiet success and today stands nearly equal to our Republic's storied NASA in its capabilities and achievements.

Other existing institutions ought openly to acknowledge their confederative nature; in so doing, they will be compelled to reckon with the limitations and imperatives inherent to such a form of association and to reform themselves where they are deficient. Moreover, collaborations that today are governed only by static treaty, and so rely on their signatories to remain consistent without regard to their domestic political upheavals, could in some cases be improved if they are recast as institutions of this sort. Trade, in particular, could benefit from such reform: the North American Free Trade Agreement might have avoided full renegotiation had it, through regular revision by its members' representatives, been able to respond incrementally to the popular will.

We further propose that our Union seek to found new institutions upon these principles wherever foreign collaboration would advance a common interest more effectively than national action alone.[235] For such institutions to be entered into voluntarily, they might need to allow a degree of flexibility. The European Union possesses this quality in rudimentary form: there is membership in the European Economic Area, which carries one set of privileges and obligations; membership in the union itself, which carries another; and for the most committed, adoption of the euro. Such variations in commitment, whereby a joining country chooses which aspects of its sovereignty it will limit in exchange for gaining certain benefits from an institution, can and ought to be formalized in the institution's founding treaty; countries may therefore join without having to make a leap of faith. Once inside such a 'multi-speed confederation,' as this concept is becoming known,[236] a country, seeing the benefit membership brings, might decide to increase its commitment to the institution thereafter; and so much the better if it does, for unity bolsters an institution's potency, advancing the interests of all within.

The question of fairly assessing contributions to an institution's governing body, often the source of considerable controversy, also admits of a simple solution in several cases: the institution ought to be so designed that the share of votes each member possesses in it is in proportion to the contribution the member makes to the institution's sustenance, whether the contribution consists of funds, facilities, personnel, or services.[237] That this method reduces the influence of small and poor nations in such institutions is to some extent true, and in certain cases it might be appropriate to balance weighted votes in some areas with equal votes in others; but in general, as it is small and poor countries which benefit the most from international institutions, proportional voting is a just aspect for such confederations. The World Bank is a successful example of this dynamic: wealthy countries hold greater sway in its decisions, but poor ones reap a greater relative benefit from its projects.

The notion that contributions can consist not only in funds, but also in items that advance the common goal, applies particularly to military collaborations. It is often the case therein that members who face the least immediate threat ride on the expenses of those who bear the primary military burden. Exhortation and, at last resort, the threat of exclusion are a partial remedy in such cases; yet they might be more usefully accompanied with demands for specific capabilities rather than for a fixed expenditure of funds. Such an approach allows reluctant members to be inventive in their contribution and to align it with some other particular interest, such as the advancement of a domestic industry, which can also serve the common aim.

We must lastly add a note, perhaps obvious, that international institutions function more effectively when they are formed with friendly nations. China and Russia are unlikely to join our Republic in a new institution unless their aim is merely to stymie it, as they so often do to the United

Nations.[238] Our Union shall sooner find success if it focuses on improving its cooperation with fellow republics, especially those with whom it has much in common, such as the members of the former British Commonwealth,[239] or if it builds upon existing leagues with the potential to be invigorated, such as the Organization of American States. Republics, in the long run, are more reliable partners in international endeavors,[240] and ties of language and history ease collaboration.

So is it that our Union could address those great works which it alone cannot solve, and reliably maintain influence abroad, in a manner quite recognizable to its people from its resemblance to their own history and principles, by reforming and building upon the system of international institutions which exists at present. All shall not be achieved in a day, but our Republic ought at once to start the task of reforming its world order; challenges to all mankind await resolution, to which we shall turn our attention in our next and final essay.

No. 13 – On Great Works

That human civilization must grow and expand – That mankind must conserve the natural world as it extends its dominion – That conservation must admit the needs of human progress – That global warming ought to be halted and reversed – That humans ought to explore outer space and settle new worlds – That conservation and exploration support the general welfare of the Union – That policies for them ought to work with the free market and local governments – That a tax on carbon emissions ought to be enacted – That geo-engineering ought to be considered – That the Moon ought to be revisited and Mars reached – That ethics and foresight must accompany new technologies – That our Union may work with Russia in exploration and China in conservation

"For more than three years I have spoken about the New Frontier. This is not a partisan term and it is not the exclusive property of Republicans or Democrats. It refers, instead, to this Nation's place in history, to the fact that we do stand on the edge of a great new era, filled with both crisis and opportunity, an era to be characterized by achievement and by challenge. It is an era which calls for action and for the best efforts of all those who would test the unknown and the uncertain in every phase of human endeavor. It is a time for pathfinders and pioneers." —**John F. Kennedy, speech dedicating the Aerospace Medical Health Center, Nov. 21st, 1963.**

In our previous essay, we offered a reform of international institutions so as to harness the collective might of several countries toward achieving the great works of this century. In this, our final essay, we shall elaborate on the foremost of those works: the conservation of the Earth, the exploration and settlement of outer space, and the development of new technologies that could either expand or constrain the sovereignty of mankind. Their importance arises from fundamental principles of morality, and their urgency from self-interest. For we, as people, must either finish these tasks or else someday the consequences of having left them undone will finish us;[241] and our best chance to advance them is now, in the present. We therefore call for action, and shall here propose several means by which these great tasks may be accomplished.

It is the nature of human society to grow and expand; in fact, to do so is imperative to our survival. We cannot rely for our well-being on the mercy of some yet-undiscovered alien race nor on the unfeeling mechanisms of nature, which might through some disaster one day ruin the Earth and all upon it.[242] Thus, just as republics must expand their power and influence in the world to secure their liberty from the exactions of a conqueror, so must the civilization of all mankind expand its power and influence in the universe to preserve all which we as people hold dear.[243] For though it is the nature of life that we never entirely control our fate, by expanding beyond one planet we may nonetheless extend the control we do have and so increase the likelihood of our continued existence and independence. We are made for action, and passivity does not befit us, or else we would have remained content to be prey for lions and wolves and would never have crafted the tools that allowed us to overcome them and achieve our present supremacy on Earth.

Yet if while expanding in this world and beyond it we ravage everything we touch, then we are but a race of parasites, undeserving of such empire. Our nations must grow in might and wealth, but we must govern them justly, or else we are not civilized, but barbarians; likewise, our population and the industry to support it must grow, but we must also conserve all that we can of nature. Conservation is in this way a moral duty.[244] As mankind expands into outer space, we must conserve, as best we can in accordance with our needs, the natural state of the worlds we settle.

This logic may seem to create a paradox. Man has a duty both to expand and to conserve, yet the two are in some ways inherently opposed, for in every place where man is present, nature is affected. This is true, and thus the conservationism we uphold necessarily differs from certain environmentalist creeds which argue that the greater good can be served only through mankind ceding the dominance it has heretofore attained over nature. Such a philosophy, which calls for humanity to live primitively and shrink in population, is an invitation to man's extinction and we reject it; so too do we reject the disproportionate obstruction of human progress for narrow ecological concerns.[245]

Rather, both duties – advancement of civilization and

conservation of nature – must be taken seriously, and a balance struck between them. This notion is not paradoxical if examined closely. Mankind, after all, depends on natural resources; those resources are sustained by the Earth itself, which is of such complexity that the ruin of a small part can cause the depletion of a much wider section; and so a failure to conserve as much of the natural world as practical will ultimately result in the exhaustion of resources on which civilization depends, thus causing hardship for future generations.[246] Our guiding principle, therefore, is to not be wasteful.[247] Mankind ought not to deprive itself of what it needs, but it ought to use only what it needs; and it ought to use the things it needs for as long as they can be used before discarding them. On this principle, our Union set aside great areas of wilderness in the 20th century while also improving agriculture and industry so as to draw more resources from less land, and it widely succeeded in this regard.

In this 21st century, however, it is not the management of land that is of primary concern, but rather the management of the Earth's atmosphere. Of all the matters of conservation, there is none today of such dire and urgent consequence as the phenomenon of global warming.[248] It is even now causing the polar ice to melt, the sea to rise, and fire to spread. To avert the dangers that this chaos presents to our civilization, and to show mankind's fitness to rule on Earth and expand into the universe, we must halt this menace and repair the damage it has already caused.

Human industry brought this threat upon the Earth; human ingenuity can surely overcome it; and today the sole question is whether human will can be summoned to meet it. A sordid few, who pursue their immediate and private interests ahead of the well-being of their Republic, have sought actively to obstruct this object. They have been aided in this pursuit by skepticism among the public. This quality, insofar as its general function is to scrutinize authority, can ordinarily be counted as an essential republican virtue, but in this instance it is liable to result in negligent inaction. To those who doubt that global warming is occurring, we say to go north and witness it yourself: it has reshaped the land, leaving only rocks and dirt where great bodies of ice stood not forty years before. To those who doubt its human cause, we say that mankind ought to confront it nonetheless. Humanity is bound both to conserve the natural world and to attain mastery over it; if you do not see this matter as the former, you ought to see it as the latter. Nature has bestowed on us a free will. If this menace to our world was initiated by nature, let man and woman end it.[249]

Having so established the logic that leads us to our ends, we shall now endeavor to define them more clearly. First, our Union ought immediately to slow and then to halt global warming. The first step toward this goal is for the United States to rejoin the Paris Accord and make good its promises therein; and the main effect of doing so shall be to demonstrate to other nations that our Republic means to do its part, and expects them to do theirs. Yet the terms of that agreement, even if faithfully adhered to, are insufficient to the task at hand. Further effort shall doubtlessly be needed, and even then the task will not end once warming is only halted. Our Union's next aim, by century's end, ought to be to restore the world to the temperatures it averaged in the middle part of the past century, prior to the acceleration of warming that marked the start of the present crisis. Over a longer period, the aim ought to be to restore, as far as practicable, the atmospheric conditions that existed prior to the Industrial Revolution, and thereby rectify the harm that mankind has wrought on the Earth through the industrial emission of carbon dioxide.

Second, the United States, in cooperation with other countries, ought to chart the universe with the aim of discovering habitable planets; then, on developing the necessary technical ability, it ought to send human astronauts to explore and ultimately to settle them. The obvious first steps toward this end are for U.S. astronauts to return to the Moon and thenceforth journey to Mars.[250] Although those destinations are not themselves likely to yield immediate and tangible benefits, the act of reaching them shall advance our Republic toward the more distant and rewarding ambition. Voyages to the Moon and Mars will, out of necessity, prompt advances in spaceflight and in the sustenance of astronauts on distant travels; and those locations, once infrastructure is constructed on them, may serve as waypoints for fueling and provisioning further exploration.[251]

These goals are, in the long term, mutually supporting: in shifting some population and industry off the Earth, the pressure on this planet will ease. In the interim, they require sustained effort on a grand scale, which can be done only with the combined resources and authority of many nations. Nature does not recognize human boundaries, nor do the consequences that result if its maintenance is neglected. It is thus necessary and proper that final authority in our Republic for conservation and exploration rest with the federal government, for those matters are vital to the general welfare of the United States. Our Union ought also, when necessary, to confer some authority over these affairs upon international bodies that satisfy the criteria in our previous essay.

That federal and international bodies ought to direct such efforts, however, does not mean that the policies made to attain them ought to be monolithic. Rather, as excessively centralized approaches are ineffective as a general rule, it is best that higher governments allow some local discretion in the particulars of implementation. Nor should policies ignore or run contrary to the workings of the free market, because they would then be wasteful and doomed to eventual failure. Instead, any public plan ought to make use of the flexibility and innovation of private enterprise and ought to be structured so as to encourage such enterprise, rather than stifle it.

Ultimately, the tide will turn on global warming when it becomes profitable for industry, without subsidy, to mass-produce clean energy;[252] the next era of space exploration will begin in earnest when a technological breakthrough allows for rapid manned spaceflight. Yet efforts can and ought to be made now to prepare for and encourage those shifts. To that end, we propose that projects related to these great works be prioritized in the ordinary allocation of federal funds for research and development.[253] Support to research, if it is properly accounted for, functions as an investment rather than a subsidy: it is needed only until a breakthrough is reached, and any breakthrough has the potential to produce a return far greater than the original investment.

As regards global warming, we second the proposal, already made from several quarters, for a tax on the emission of carbon.[254] If such a tax is of substance but not excessive, it could alter the calculations of energy firms such that they do a public good by investing in clean fuels while continuing to grow their business. Contrast this approach to a ban on dirty energy. A prohibition would bankrupt companies for a reason unrelated to their competitiveness, which is both callous and foolish. It would wrong their employees by suddenly casting them out of work, and it would surrender the world market to foreign firms that are unbound by any limitation on the amount of carbon they may emit. Contrast it, too, with a subsidy for clean energy, which would drain public funds to keep uncompetitive firms in business. A moderate carbon tax shall instead divert competitive enterprises into new channels of industry, while collecting public revenue to invest in research.

To repair the damage caused by global warming, however, it is not sufficient to produce clean energy now: the world has already warmed, and vast swathes of the Arctic, and to a lesser extent the Antarctic, have melted and cannot be retrieved by a reduction of emissions. Indeed, since the polar regions have warmed faster than the rest of the world, and as carbon dioxide lingers in the skies for decades or more, they would continue to thaw even if mankind ceased its emissions today; and because the polar ice itself has so far slowed the planet's warming by reflecting sunlight from its surface, its further deterioration will only exacerbate the world's plight. Yet its recovery, if achieved, shall in the same manner speed the recovery of the entire Earth.

When wisdom fails, ingenuity must be resorted to. Therefore, to restore the Earth to what it was and ought still to be, we propose the use of geo-engineering: in this case, action to cool the polar regions by removing carbon directly from the atmosphere using human inventions. Such an attempt, it is claimed by some, would constitute a dangerous and unprecedented intervention by mankind in the affairs of nature. Yet this claim overlooks the truth that global warming is itself geo-engineering on a vast scale, albeit unwitting; and the fact that it is unintended, and thus uncontrolled, renders it far more dangerous to man and nature than a deliberate, limited effort to cure the blight it has wrought. Technologies employed to this end ought to be studied carefully and tested incrementally, lest they produce unintended effects, and their development and use ought, so far as practical, to be in concert with other countries. Nonetheless, geo-engineering offers mankind a way to heal the world that we as people know and cherish; its use ought not to be shunned.

As for space exploration, it is first necessary that the United States regain the ability to send astronauts to space. It is poor policy, not only for our Union but for the world, to rely solely on the Russian government to convey mankind into the cosmos. Our Republic, being as it is the greatest world power, has long had the capacity to right this deficiency; recently, it has lacked only the will.[255] NASA's Orion spacecraft and Space Launch System, which were once intended to replace the Space Shuttle upon its retirement in 2011, ought to be made spaceworthy without further delay; so, too, ought the spacecraft being built on contract by private American firms.

Indeed, NASA need not explore outer space entirely on its own: our Republic is home to several private enterprises that seek opportunity beyond the bounds of the Earth. The federal government ought to work with them as it did with the railroad firms during our Union's western expansion, and as Britain did by granting royal charters in its early days of American settlement. The U.S. government ought to persist in employing such companies to launch its satellites; it is right to contract them to build a new generation of spacecraft; and it ought to aid in insuring their efforts to develop the final frontier, replete as those ventures shall be with financial risk. Moreover, just as the Royal Navy protected the settlement of the Thirteen Colonies, and as the U.S. Cavalry guarded the routes West, so ought the U.S. military today to redouble its efforts to protect American and allied interests beyond Earth. We thus endorse the proposal, advanced by the present administration, to establish a military service responsible for operations in space.

Here we must recall, however, the principled argument for partial privatization that we made in an earlier essay. NASA must have its own means of accessing outer space, or else its contractors shall, in the spirit of oligopoly, come to offer poor services for exacting prices. To avoid complete redundancy, however, labor ought to be divided – as, wisely, is now being done. NASA is right to focus on exploring the distant reaches of space, in which it may invest the superior resources of government, whereas private firms ought to develop routes and resources nearer to Earth, in which their greater efficiency may bring both public and private benefit.

So, too, ought our Union and its fellow republics to deliberate on how new worlds, once explored, shall be governed. It will be to the eternal credit of mankind if our most enlightened forms of government are the ones which we extend beyond the Earth; but it will be to mankind's eternal shame if we instead extend those which are the most tyrannical. In view of this consideration, it is significant that republics are not the only nations engaged in space exploration. China, which makes no pretense of its despotism, has made substantial progress in this field, such that it threatens to overtake the United States by being the first to land human explorers on Mars. Our Republic ought not to yield the initiative, but rather seize the opportunity to compete. It ought to return its astronauts to the Moon forthwith, before China's arrive there; and by the time China lands its pioneers on the Moon, our Union's ought already to be on their way to Mars. We thus endorse wholeheartedly NASA's Artemis plan, whose object is to return Americans to the Moon in 2024; and we expect that that venerable institution will soon thereafter turn its sights to Mars.

As our Republic and other countries labor on the great works of this century, however, they must soberly weigh the means they employ. The development of new technologies that alter the possibilities of human society cannot reasonably be shunned, nor should it be. It is at the core of human nature to inquire and experiment, and the inventions that result from this activity, when guided by common ethics, have been and shall continue to be of immense benefit to mankind. Yet blind faith in technology, and the reckless and unethical development of it, is one of the greatest follies that man is liable to fall into, and it is one which may yet bring humanity's destruction. Advances in two areas, artificial intelligence and human genetics, warrant concern on this count. The former, if pursued uncritically, risks ceding mankind's control over its own fate; the latter risks placing in mankind's hands far more control over its fate than it ought ever to have.

In designing machines which are ever more capable and aware, we must beware that they could replace us: either swiftly and violently, as in the horror stories of science fiction, or slowly and peacefully, as we, in indolence, neglect to think or to work for ourselves. To prevent such an occurrence, our

Republic ought to employ the same means to limit the power of robots that it has long used to limit the power of men: dividing authority among independent bodies, instituting checks and balances between them, and establishing laws that limit the extent to which power may be exercised. We thus propose that artificial intelligence never be given full autonomy over weapons that can be used to slaughter humans,[256] and that this restriction be codified in law. We further propose that reasonable limits to the interconnectivity of various items over the internet be established, so that no single artificial intelligence is afforded the opportunity to infiltrate an unlimited array of devices which it could employ to effect a sudden coup.

In the case of genetics, if people were to be given a discretionary and unlimited ability to alter their genes or those of their offspring, disaster would certainly follow. Even if the risk of gruesome defects caused by the unforeseen effects of such meddling could be eliminated, mankind, in its rush to usurp the prerogatives of nature by seeking a flawed ideal of perfection, would edit out of existence the natural diversity that enables our species to thrive. Humanity would become monochrome and stagnant; though the friction that comes with difference would fade, so would the flashes of brilliance that result from it. Bereft of such dynamism, civilization would decline. We therefore propose that gene-altering technology ought to be used on humans only in cases of severe need, and only as a last resort;[257] and that laws be passed prohibiting such technology from being made available, on any account, for cosmetic or eugenic purposes.

Several other technologies with potential for misuse no doubt exist, but it is beyond our scope to identify and expound on them all; we say only that our Republic ought to apply ethics and foresight to each. Yet it will be of little use that there are laws governing such technologies in the United States if our Union fails to maintain itself as a leading inventor of them. China has declared its intention to compete with our Republic in this regard, and it has so far used its advances not for the common good of mankind, but for the oppression of its citizens. It is thus a moral imperative, somewhat in tension with itself, for our Republic both to regulate carefully its own inventions and to compete effectively with its rivals, who almost certainly shall not regulate theirs. To reconcile and thereby fulfill these parallel ends, we urge our Union to press its natural advantages in education, openness, and critical thought, which are the foundations of invention.

Finally, though we caution against dependence on them or unwarranted trust in their good intentions, there does exist some potential for our Union, as a gesture of common humanity and goodwill, to cooperate with its two foremost adversaries on the great works of conservation and exploration. At the end of the Cold War, the United States began a joint endeavor in space with Russia. Together, they built the International Space Station that several countries use today; and despite the present tension between the two on Earth, well-warranted on account of Russian encroachments, their combined efforts in space have proceeded constructively. China, though it is a declared rival in space, may prove an able partner to our Republic in halting global warming on Earth. The government in Beijing has suffered the ills of environmental damage at home and so has some interest in addressing matters of conservation that affect the world. It is reasonable for the United States and China to work together in that field for the common good, and thereby balance the rivalry that shall otherwise mark their relations in this century.

Mankind needs a frontier in which to constructively expend its energies;[258] it also needs a home, consistent and recognizable, that it may treasure and from time to time withdraw to.[259] By rejecting passivity and setting our minds to great works, we can reopen the frontier and preserve our home. This essay will nonetheless feel incomplete, for to fully craft the policies necessary to attain its goals requires technical knowledge that we here do not possess. Yet we have endeavored to identify vital ends, to explain the moral logic behind them, and to offer some proposals that we consider to have a chance of success and that are consistent with principles expressed elsewhere in this series. We thus ask you, fellow citizens: What shall you leave to your grandchildren?

The Past, The Present, and The Future

"If one wishes a Republic to live long, it is necessary to draw it back often towards its beginning."
—**Niccolò Machiavelli,** ***Discourses on Titus Livy*, 1517.**

In thirteen essays, we have endeavored to present a political perspective founded anew on the principles of the Enlightenment and not bound to the worn refrains of the two major parties. We began with statements of principle, followed with arguments for governance, economics, and foreign affairs, and ended with a vision of what mankind may yet achieve. We yearn to see the United States resurgent, renewed as an enlightened Republic, working in concert with other free nations to preserve liberty and defeat tyranny; we desire to see it as a mighty Union that extends beyond the bounds of the Earth, yet in which each man and woman is represented in government and in most affairs is left at liberty to govern him- or herself as he or she sees fit; and we wish to see it as a federation of States, in which the preponderance of affairs that cannot responsibly be left to individual discretion are instead decided at a level of government closest to the people.

If this rhetoric carries a familiar echo, that is because it merely restates what our Union's Founders intended for our nation.[260] It is no revelation; it is simply a new ordering of venerable ideas. Yet it is the nature of things that these ideas, and the Republic they carry, are perpetually in danger of neglect. Neglect, over decades, causes pillars to crumble; and a damaged house can only endure so many blows from man and fortune till it shall collapse.

These United States have now for several years been assailed by the insidious delusion of illiberal democracy, an idea of man that this series of essays was conceived to rebut. The result of that struggle lies undecided ahead of us. Yet our Union is now subjected to another assault, by a disease borne on the winds of fortune and colliding with a house divided and in disrepair.

We cannot offer policy to contain and defeat this virus; that must come from the men and women who have dedicated their lives to the study of medicine, and be implemented with due care by those whom the public has at present entrusted with civic authority. We shall only urge our fellow citizens to keep faith with the cause of liberty. In this trial, some might look with envy on the effort of a foreign government, centralized and totalitarian, to halt the disease; and they, afraid, might wonder whether such a system of government could better shield its citizens from the ravages of fortune. To this, we say that totalitarianism allowed the contagion to spread, for, in keeping with its ordinary mode, it silenced those who were first to speak.

In these United States, which encountered the virus at a more advanced stage, a different pattern has so far emerged; and though it is a very imperfect one, it gives some cause for hope. A federal response, more concerted and coherent than that to date, would be necessary and proper in such a crisis and certainly desired. Yet, in the absence of it, the States and cities have begun to act vigorously and on their own initiative. It will be through their effort, as much as the effort of the center, that our Union shall emerge from the present emergency; and it will be through their effort, likewise, that our Republic may emerge revitalized from its present political turmoil.

For a fundamental flaw in the concentration of power, the defining trait of totalitarianism and centralization, is that for it to function benignly in times of crisis it presupposes that the center shall be helmed by a wise and virtuous ruler, yet such an occurrence has throughout history been more exception than rule; whereas a fundamental strength in the diffusion of power, the defining trait of republicanism and federalism, is that among a large body of people there will always be some who are wise and virtuous, and those will obtain at least some power and do good with it.

Indeed, though much may yet intrude between the moment of this writing and the coming presidential election, it appears as if our Union might gain a reprieve. Mr. Biden, as much as we disagree with him on many matters of policy, is no peddler of illiberal democracy. We reckon that his accession to the Presidency, should it transpire, shall have a calming effect on the Republic.

Yet if this were to occur, and even if the virus, too, were to subside, it shall nonetheless be imperative on both counts that the citizens of these United States remain vigilant. Just as the virus might find some hidden reservoir amidst humanity, where it may silently dwell and from time to time savagely resurface until it is finally eradicated, likewise has illiberal democracy crept into a dark recess in our Union's consciousness. Each time it rears its head it shall have to be vanquished, or our Republic will be lost to despotism. Fellow citizens, our country's trial shall not soon be over; rather, it is just begun.

And that is just as well, for what is needed now is not the promise of an instantaneous resolution, but hard, honest work. None of the ideals presented in this series shall be realized in a day; they might take decades to attain, and some might never be fulfilled entirely. Nor, even if our proposals could by some stroke of luck all be implemented at once, should they be. We are but human. Some of the policies we have put forth may, in the fullness of time, prove to possess some unforeseen flaw; others, which might prove fruitful over years, could nonetheless cause harm if enacted too suddenly or without great care. It is better, then, for them to appear as one argument in our Republic's civic debate, so that they may be challenged and tested by those skeptical of them, and that they may emerge as law or policy only as the product of deliberation and compromise.

But the ideas are worthwhile; they shall, in time, produce results far better than those that would result from autocracy or the dim contradiction of 'illiberal democracy,' and thus we believe unwaveringly that a new model of classical federalism is worth striving for. So strive we shall.

This project, in the words of James Madison, is not the offspring of a single brain. It is only begun with these essays, composed over four years of conversation and deliberation with a number of patriotic citizens, and by the time of its fulfillment it will be the work of many heads and many hands.[261] We call for the formation of a great American political party to rival the two that presently exist, or to

claim a place in the two-party system that is today occupied by one of them. We ask for scholars to read, consider, and refine our arguments, for statesmen to guide us through the chambers of government, and for you, fellow citizens, to support this undertaking through the continuous exercise of your fundamental rights of citizenship in the years to come.
—A humble Citizen, March 29, 2020

Afterword

Originally published as a blog post titled "The Danger Is Not Yet Past" on January 24th, 2021, four days after the inauguration of President Joseph R. Biden, Jr. and eighteen days after the attempt on the Capitol of January 6th.

I

"It is quite impossible to think of glory. Both mind and feelings are exhausted. I am wretched even at the moment of victory, and I always say that next to a battle lost, the greatest misery is a battle gained."
—The Duke of Wellington, after the Battle of Waterloo.

Mr. Trump has left the Presidency, and thus the most immediate and dire menace to our Republic has departed from the stage. But he leaves behind a broken scene.

The Capitol was overrun, and the city of Washington turned into a military camp; cities across the Union smolder after a summer of protest collapsed into the smoke of anarchy and reprisals; four hundred thousand lie dead from disease; and many millions more have been drawn into a sinister delusion that assails the very basis of republican government, confidence in a free and fair election.

Extremists, once obscure, have risen to prominence: on the right, depraved militants laying a false and perverted claim to the traditions and principles of these United States strive after civil war, seeking to intimidate elected officials and do violence to lawful government; on the left, would-be revolutionaries inculcated with an unforgiving and absolutist ideology seek to purge from public life and private employment all those who fail to recite their slogans.

None of these calamities were present in such strength in 2016. They gathered force during the presidency of Mr. Trump, and in 2020 they crashed down upon us. His selfish malice drove those demons on as they danced in our Union's fields and streets, until he himself, exposed as the tyrant he always wished to become, stood at the head of an insurrection against the elected representatives of these United States.

Yet our Republic still stands, and, as Mr. Trump fades, the Covid-19 epidemic recedes, and some measure of prosperity and competent governance returns, it may soon appear to recover.

However—

II

> "For it [the Roman agrarian law] found the power of its adversaries redoubled, and because of this it inflamed so much hatred between the plebs and the Senate that they came to arms and bloodshed, beyond every civil mode and custom. So, since the public magistrates could not remedy it, and none of the factions could put hope in them, they had recourse to private remedies, and each one of the

> parties was thinking of how to make itself a head to defend it."
>
> "In this scandal and disorder the plebs came first and gave reputation to Marius, so that it made him consul four times; and he continued in his consulate, with a few intervals, so long that he was able to make himself consul three other times. As the nobility had no remedy against such a plague, it turned to favoring Sulla; and when he had been made head of its party, they came to civil wars. After much bloodshed and changing of fortune, the nobility was left on top."
>
> "Later, these humors were revived at the time of Caesar and Pompey; for after Caesar had made himself head of Marius's party, and Pompey that of Sulla, in coming to grips Caesar was left on top. He was the first tyrant in Rome, such that never again was that city free." —**Niccolò Machiavelli,** ***Discourses on Titus Livy,*** **Bk. 1, Ch. 37.**

The Roman Republic did not fall in a day, nor upon the first attempt to overthrow it. It began to decay after its final triumph over Carthage, in 146 B.C. At that moment, Rome stood mighty and unchallenged, but its leaders grew arrogant and its people complacent. They quarreled bitterly amongst themselves and became frightened whenever some passing foreign menace appeared on the horizon; thus, they began to disregard their customs in their search for safety or advantage.[262] In 91 B.C., unrest and revolt broke out across Italy amongst those whom Rome had neglected in its years of triumph, and the Romans only with difficulty suppressed them.[263]

But it was in the decade after 88 B.C. that the pillars of the Republic took the first of the blows that would fell them. Marius and Sulla, each at the head of a faction and each in their turn, briefly grasped at unchecked power and attempted the wholesale destruction of their enemies. The old traditions and customs that upheld the Roman constitution buckled under their ceaseless assaults. The law became a dead letter, discarded when it did not suit their purposes. They demanded absolute and abject loyalty from their fellow senators, the tribunes of the people, and other distinguished citizens; they purged those who did not give it.

Their rule did not last, but neither was held accountable. Marius died of old age while still clinging to power. Sulla, to the surprise of all, laid down his dictatorship, retired to his villa, and, after a year of debauchery, died in his bed. His fade from power and public life was swift, and for nearly twenty years the Republic appeared restored.

But two young men had witnessed his example, that selfishness and force opened a path to power. Caesar and Pompey were more intelligent, diligent, and disciplined than Marius and Sulla; and so, when they clashed, Rome shook even more violently. Caesar emerged victorious, but in 44 B.C. he was assassinated by a fallen Senate desperate to reclaim its lawful powers.

Yet two more young men were watching. Antony and Octavian rose to power and then came to blows. Octavian, like Caesar his uncle, was disciplined and brilliant; unlike Caesar, he was wholly ruthless. In 27 B.C. he became the Emperor Augustus and reigned for forty years. Only then did the Roman Republic cease finally to exist.

III

"...consider whether in a corrupt city one can maintain a free state, if there is one, or, if it has not been there, whether one can order it. On this thing I say that it is very difficult to do either the one or the other... For as good customs have need of laws to maintain themselves, so laws have need of good customs so as to be observed. Besides this, the orders and laws made in a republic at its birth, when men were good, are no longer to the purpose later, when they have become wicked." —**Niccolò Machiavelli,** ***Discourses on Titus Livy*, Bk. 1, Ch. 18.**

The politics of the Roman Republic were generally bloodier and more tumultuous than our own, and Rome had a much different constitution; thus, any comparison between the two is necessarily imperfect. Yet it would be foolhardy not to contemplate the possibility that Mr. Trump was our Sulla. He disregarded every law, custom, and tradition that stood in his path; he proscribed anyone who crossed him; and he recklessly stoked the violence of the mob. Then he left office, still living. And, most crucially, he has so far not been held to account.

Congress, had it any vigor or authority remaining to it, would have impeached and removed Mr. Trump on January 6th, immediately upon reclaiming the Capitol. The Senate may still limp to such a conclusion, months later; though it appears to me that each passing day makes this outcome less likely, as what little resolve was summoned on that night dissolves into cowardice and irresolution. Whichever young men and women would be our Caesar and Octavian, more diligent and ruthless than Mr. Trump, are watching this scene. They will take note of how it ends.

Yet the failures of the people's representatives must ultimately be laid at the feet of the people themselves. We elect our leaders, and, if we wish to avert the fate that befell Rome, so must we be the ones to demand virtue from them and uphold it with our votes. And we shall only recognize virtue in our candidates for public office if we know and practice it ourselves. Do you? Do I?

IV

> "A republic has need of new acts of foresight every day if one wishes to maintain it free." —**Niccolò Machiavelli,** *Discourses on Titus Livy*, **Bk. 3, Ch. 49.**

Although our national stage is battered, the inauguration of Mr. Biden, should he carry through the assurances of moderation that he has made on campaign, offers us citizens an opportunity to pause and take our eyes away from it. His actions there will neither save nor destroy the Republic. That will hinge on whether we, in this interim, can rediscover civic virtue.

The place to do so is in our towns, counties, cities, and States. In writing this series of essays, I came to the theoretical conclusion that we as citizens can take part in and see our hand in the results of local government far more than we can in the government of the Union.

Subsequent experience has, for me, confirmed the truth of

that proposition. The essays comprising the core of this work, which deal with national issues, are but a drop in the ocean; few shall read them, because there exist thousands of other written works that, for good or ill, ponder the challenges of the United States. Yet in the span of little more than a year, and despite the obstacle of Covid-19, I have already found a modest place in the civic life of my adopted town.

It is there, at the level of government that is most accessible to us, that we may take an active part in governing and so become reacquainted with, and practiced in, civic virtue: attachment, respect, duty, honor, foresight, patience, hard work, collaboration, persuasion, compromise, leadership. Once we have taught ourselves these qualities in the gymnasium of local government, then we may apply them to our national contests and so repair our Republic.

So, let us relax our minds during the next few weeks, as the tension of the past four years gradually unwinds. Then let us seize the opportunity now offered and begin to work.

* * *

> "Nor is it out of place to mention such testimonies in the case of a man said to have been by nature so fond of raillery, that when he was still young and obscure he spent much time with actors and buffoons and shared their dissolute life; and when he had made himself supreme master, he would daily assemble the most reckless stage and theatre folk to drink and bandy jests with them, although men thought that he disgraced his years, and although he not only

dishonoured his high office, but neglected much that required attention."

"...In others he seems to have been of very uneven character, and at variance with himself; he robbed much, but gave more; bestowed his honours unexpectedly, as unexpectedly his insults; fawned on those he needed, but gave himself airs towards those who needed him; so that one cannot tell whether he was more inclined by nature to disdain or flattery."
—**Plutarch,** ***Parallel Lives of Famous Greeks and Romans*****, writing of Sulla.**

Acknowledgments

As I have said before, this work cannot, and ought not to, be considered the product of a single mind working in isolation. I have authored it; but I, like all others, am to a very great extent shaped by my surroundings: by history, the world, my country, and the States and towns in which I have lived; by my forebears, family, friends, teachers, and co-workers; and, when I served in the Army, by my soldiers, sergeants, and fellow officers. Regardless of how the people I have known might feel about the contents of this work – and there is, no doubt, much scope for respectful disagreement – they have all left their mark on my character and my philosophy, and I am grateful for it. I hope to meet and learn from many more in the future.

There are some individuals whose thoughts and advice have been particularly valuable to me over the past few years as I have composed this series of essays. They do not all necessarily agree with or endorse every proposal contained within the series; but, considering this work to be a sincere effort motivated by a love of country that they all share, they took the time to read my drafts – sometimes repeatedly – and give me suggestions to improve them. I cannot be the judge of my own work, but I can say with certainty that their input has made this series far better than it would have been without them. All remaining errors, in fact or judgment, are fully my own.

Thus, I give my sincere thanks to my brother, Andrew Caves; to my father, John P. Caves, Jr.; to my father-in-law, Peter DiGasbarro; and to my friends Brent Dickinson and Joshua Sandler. I also thank my sister-in-law, Diana DiGasbarro, for volunteering her time and skill to design the cover for this book. More than any other, I am deeply grateful to my dear friend Matthew Sanyour, who has worked closely with me on this project from its inception five years ago and whose wise advice has been indispensable. Likewise has been the advice, love, and patience of my wife Christina. There are others who have asked not to be mentioned by name here, and they have my gratitude as well. I owe a great debt to them all.

Bibliography

Although most of the works, speeches, and letters I refer to throughout this work are themselves in the public domain,[264] I owe a debt of gratitude to the various translators, editors, biographers, and publishers who have made those storied words available to the modern reader. Below is a list of the editions, biographies, and other resources that I referenced while composing my essays:

Burke, Edmund. *Pre-Revolutionary Writings*. Edited by Ian Harris. Cambridge, U.K.: Cambridge University Press, 1993.

Burke, Edmund. *Revolutionary Writings*. Edited by Iain Hampsher-Monk. New York: Cambridge University Press, 2014.

Chernow, Ron. *Grant*. New York: Penguin, 2017.

Chernow, Ron. *Washington: A Life*. New York: Penguin, 2010.

Clausewitz, Carl von. *On War*. Translated and edited by Michael Howard and Peter Paret. Princeton: Princeton University Press, 1989.

Grant, Ulysses S. *Personal Memoirs*. New York: Barnes & Noble, 2003.

Hamilton, Alexander, James Madison, and John Jay. *The Federalist with Letters of "Brutus"*. Edited by Terence Ball. New York: Cambridge University Press, 2003.

Holmes, Richard. *Wellington: The Iron Duke*. London: HarperCollins, 2003.

Locke, John. *A Letter Concerning Toleration*. Edited by James H. Tully. Indianapolis: Hackett Publishing Company, 1983.

Locke, John. *Second Treatise of Government*. Edited by C. B. Macpherson. Indianapolis: Hackett Publishing Company, 1980.

Machiavelli, Niccolò. *Discourses on Livy*. Translated by Harvey C. Mansfield and Nathan Tarcov. Chicago: University of Chicago Press, 1996.

Mahan, Alfred Thayer. *The Interest of America in Sea Power, Present and Future*. Okitoks Press, 2017.

Montesquieu, Charles de Secondat, Baron of. *The Spirit of the Laws*. Edited by Anne M. Cohler, Basia C. Miller, and Harold S. Stone. New York: Cambridge University Press, 1989.

Morris, Edmund. *Theodore Rex*. New York: Random House, 2001.

Roberts, Andrew. *Churchill: Walking with Destiny*. New York: Penguin, 2018.

Rosseau, Jean-Jacques. On the Social Contract. Translated by Donald A. Cress. Indianapolis: Hackett Publishing Company, 1987.

Smith, Adam. *An Inquiry into the Nature and Causes of the Wealth of Nations*. Edited by Edwin Cannan. Chicago: University of Chicago Press, 1976.

Tocqueville, Alexis de. *Democracy in America*. Translated and edited by Harvey C. Mansfield and Delba Winthrop. Chicago: University of Chicago Press, 2000.

A special thanks to:

The Library of Congress website for making publicly available the original text of speeches and letters by George Washington, James Madison, Abraham Lincoln, Frederick Douglass, and Theodore Roosevelt, as well as the text of Alexander Hamilton's First and Second Reports on Public Credit and his Report on Manufactures.

The U.S. Census Bureau website for making publicly available population figures and estimates for the several states and territories, as well as for the United States as a whole.

The John F. Kennedy Presidential Library and Museum and the Ronald Reagan Presidential Library and Museum websites for making publicly available the original text of speeches made by John F. Kennedy and Ronald Reagan, respectively.

The University of Virginia Miller Center website for making publicly available the original text and audio of speeches made by George H. W. Bush.

The National Congress of American Indians (NCAI) website for providing useful reference material on the demographics and legal status of American Indian and Alaska Native nations.

Dr. Marjorie Bloy and her website, *A Web of English History* (http://www.historyhome.co.uk/), for making publicly available the text of various speeches made by British Members of Parliament during the Corn Laws debate.

Bill Thayer and his University of Chicago-hosted website, *LacusCurtius* (https://penelope.uchicago.edu/Thayer/E/Roman/home.html), for making publicly available the text of Plutarch's *Parallel Lives of Famous Greeks and Romans*, itself drawn from the Loeb Classical Library edition translated by Bernadotte Perrin and published in the early 20th century.

The Voices of Democracy project website, hosted by the University of Maryland (https://voicesofdemocracy.umd.edu/), for making publicly available the text of Susan B. Anthony's "Is It a Crime for a U.S. Citizen to Vote?" speech, itself drawn from *The Selected Papers of Elizabeth Cady Stanton and Susan B. Anthony, Volume II: An Aristocracy of Sex, 1866-1873* by Ann D. Gordon (New Brunswick, NJ: Rutgers University Press, 2000).

The University of Rochester Frederick Douglass Project website (https://rbscp.lib.rochester.edu/2494), for making publicly available the text of Frederick Douglass' "5th of July" speech (also known as "What to the Slave Is the Fourth of July?").

Although I have not pulled excerpts or information directly from them, I would also like to recognize *The Revenge of Geography: What the Map Tells Us About Coming Conflicts and the Battle Against Fate* by Robert D. Kaplan (New York: Random House, 2013) and *Special Providence: American Foreign Policy and How It Changed the World* by Walter Russell Mead (New York: Taylor & Francis, 2002) for being the latest in a long line of excellent works that have influenced my thinking on grand strategy and foreign policy.

About the Author

John P. Caves III is a foreign policy professional, freelance writer, community volunteer, and former Army officer. While on active duty in the U.S. Army from 2013 to 2017, he traveled across the country and lived in Alaska and Oklahoma before returning to civilian life in his home state of Maryland. He holds a bachelor's degree in Public and International Affairs from Princeton University and a master's in Global Communication from the George Washington University.

Disclaimer: The opinions, analyses, positions or other information stated by the author are the author's alone and cannot be attributed, credited, implied to, or otherwise associated with, any entity with the exception of appropriate source attribution.

In plainer language: This work was not sponsored by any organization or public figure, nor does it necessarily reflect the views of anyone other than myself, except to the extent to which my thinking has been influenced by the sources I have cited and by the friends, mentors, and family members whom I have mentioned in my acknowledgments.

Notes

FOREWORD

1   In his "5th of July" speech (known also as "What to the Slave Is the Fourth of July?") delivered in Rochester, New York, on July 5, 1852.

THE SITUATION OF THESE UNITED STATES

2   We refer here and in subsequent essays not only to a popular majority, but to any majority that bestows power within the framework of a republic's constitution. In the case of these United States, that may be an Electoral College majority or a Congressional majority, or, in certain instances, majorities within or of state legislatures.

3   "I wish you may not be going fast, and by the shortest cut, to that horrible and disgustful situation. Already there appears a poverty of conception, a coarseness and vulgarity in all the proceedings of the assembly and of all their instructors. Their liberty is not liberal. Their science is presumptuous ignorance. Their humanity is savage and brutal." Edmund Burke, *Reflections on The Revolution in France*.

NO. 1 – ON FUNDAMENTAL LIBERTIES

4   This quote was, in fact, attributed to Voltaire by a biographer; but it captures well that great man's spirit.

5   "The part of the Magistrate is only to take care that the Commonwealth receive no prejudice, and that there be no Injury done to any man, either in Life or Estate." John Locke, *A Letter Concerning Toleration*.

6   "They have taken up an idea which they seem to think quite new, but which in reality is as old as despotism and about as narrow and selfish. It has been heard and answered a thousand times over. It is the argument of the crowned heads and privileged classes of the world. It is as good against our Republican form of government as it is against the negro. The wonder is that its votaries do not see its consequences. It does away with that noble and just idea of Abraham Lincoln, that our government

should be a government of the people, by the people, and for the people, and for all the people." Frederick Douglass, "Lessons of the Hour" speech, Jan. 9, 1894.

7   "First they came for the socialists, and I did not speak out – because I was not a socialist. Then they came for the trade unionists, and I did not speak out – because I was not a trade unionist. Then they came for the Jews, and I did not speak out – because I was not a Jew. Then they came for me – and there was no one left to speak for me." Pastor Martin Niemöller, c.1946, as inscribed in the United States Holocaust Memorial Museum.

8   "The speculative line of demarcation, where obedience ought to end, and [revolutionary] resistance must begin, is faint, obscure, and not easily definable. It is not a single act, or a single event, which determines it. Governments must be abused and deranged indeed, before it can be thought of; and the prospect of the future must be as bad as the experience of the past. When things are in that lamentable condition, the nature of the disease is to indicate the remedy to those whom nature has qualified to administer in extremities this critical, ambiguous, bitter portion to a distempered state. Times and occasions, and provocations, will teach their own lessons. The wise will determine from the gravity of the case; the irritable from sensibility to oppression; the high-minded from disdain and indignation at abusive power in unworthy hands; the brave and bold from the love of honourable danger in a generous cause: but, with or without right, a revolution will be the very last resource of the thinking and the good." Edmund Burke, *Reflections on the Revolution in France*.

9   "Decline in the moral character of a people is not sudden, but gradual. The downward steps are marked at first by degrees and by increasing momentum from bad to worse." Frederick Douglass, "Lessons of the Hour" speech, Jan. 9, 1894.

10 "The Constitution only gives people the right to pursue happiness. You have to catch it yourself." This quote is attributed variously to Benjamin Franklin and Thomas Jefferson; which one, if either, said it, we do not know.

11 By the First Amendment itself. The several States may not violate the Constitution of the United States.

12 In the case of a monument on public grounds, the elected legislature of

that municipality or State; in the case of monuments on private grounds, it varies depending on the nature of the private institution concerned. For a university, for instance, we would recommend a vote of students, faculty, and alumni, though we would not dispute the right of the trustees, as the governing body, to make the decision themselves if they so choose.

13 "Who controls the past controls the future. Who controls the present controls the past." George Orwell, *1984*.

14 As in the case of an inciter of a lynch mob, or someone who stands outside a church, exhorting a crowd to ransack everything within. Inciting panic, when doing so could cause physical harm, is also justly illegal; e.g., shouting "fire" in a crowded theater. A rant by someone who calls some group by hateful names but does not threaten anyone, by contrast, is highly distasteful, but not criminal; its perpetrator ought to be shunned, but not prosecuted.

15 The result of Supreme Court precedent beginning with *New York Times v. Sullivan* in 1964 and *Curtis Publishing Co. v. Butts* in 1967.

16 "In the matter of the press there is therefore really no middle between servitude and license. To get the inestimable good that freedom of the press assures one must know how to submit to the inevitable evil it gives rise to." Alexis de Tocqueville, *Democracy in America*, Vol. 1, Part 2, Ch. 3.

17 "The sovereignty of the people and freedom of the press are therefore two entirely correlative things: censorship and universal suffrage are, on the contrary, two things that contradict each other and cannot be found in the political institutions of the same people for long." Tocqueville, *Democracy in America*, Vol. 1, Part 2, Ch. 3.

18 "To provide for calling forth the Militia to execute the Laws of the Union, suppress Insurrections and repel Invasions," *U.S. Constitution* Art. 1, Sec. 8; "The Privilege of the Writ of Habeas Corpus shall not be suspended, unless when in Cases of Rebellion or Invasion the public Safety may require it," Art. 1, Sec. 9; "…and [the United States] shall protect each of them [every State] against Invasion; and on Application of the Legislature, or of the Executive (when the Legislature cannot be convened) against domestic Violence." Art. 4, Sec. 4.

19 "Because the Care of Souls is not committed to the Civil Magistrate, any more than to other Men. It is not committed unto him, I say, by God; because it appears not that God has ever given any such Authority to

one Man over another, as to compel any one to his Religion. Nor can any such Power be vested in the Magistrate by the consent of the People; because no man can so far abandon the care of his own Salvation, as blindly to leave it to the choice of any other, whether Prince or Subject, to prescribe to him what Faith or Worship he shall embrace." John Locke, *A Letter Concerning Toleration*.

20 "But indeed if any People congregated upon account of Religion, should be desirous to sacrifice a Calf, I deny that That ought to be prohibited by a Law. Melibaeus, whose Calf it is, may lawfully kill his Calf at home and burn any part of it that he thinks fit. For no Injury is thereby done to any one, no prejudice to another man's Goods." John Locke, *A Letter Concerning Toleration*. Yet human sacrifice, for instance, as it clearly does injury to another, is logically prohibited by law.

21 Insofar as they are compelled to directly provide, pay for, or condone practices contrary to their faith; they may not, however, use the First Amendment to justify a refusal to pay general taxes on the basis that the government uses revenue from those taxes to fund or provide some such service which contradicts that citizen's faith. In that case the payment is from the citizen to the government; the government then spends that revenue on whatever the will of the majority, as expressed through Congress, lawfully demands. The Congress thus takes on the moral considerations of the spending decision; the citizen is fulfilling only his or her lawful obligation to provide revenue to the government.

22 "The preamble of the Federal Constitution says: 'We, the people of the United States, in order to form a more perfect union, establish justice, insure domestic tranquility, provide for the common defence, promote the general welfare, and secure the blessings of liberty to ourselves and our posterity, do ordain and establish this Constitution for the United States of America.' It was we the people – not we white male citizens – nor yet we male citizens – but we the whole people, who formed this Union; and we formed it, not to give the blessings of liberty, but to secure them – not to the half of ourselves and the half of our posterity, but to the whole people, women as well as men." Susan B. Anthony, "Is It a Crime for a U.S. Citizen to Vote?" speech, Apr. 3, 1873.

NO. 2 – ON FEDERALISM

23 "I speak of the federal republic. This form of government is an agreement, by which many political bodies consent to become citizens of the larger

state they want to form. It is a society of societies that make a new one, which can be enlarged by new associates that unite with it. ...This sort of republic, able to withstand external force, can be maintained at its size without internal corruption; the form of this society curbs every drawback." Montesquieu, *Spirit of the Laws*, Bk. 9, Ch. 1. In *Federalist No. 9*, Alexander Hamilton explains how the United States fits this description of government, and how a federal system not only eases the burdens of governing a large and varied territory, but safeguards liberty by reducing the field for demagoguery and limiting the scope for the exercise of tyranny.

24 Such as the direct provision of pensions (Social Security) to individual citizens under the New Deal. We elaborate in later essays.

25 "Two very distinct kinds of centralization exist... To concentrate the power to direct the [interests common to all parts of the nation] in the same place or in the same hand is to found what I shall call governmental centralization. To concentrate the power to direct the [interests special to certain parts of the nation] in the same manner is to found what I shall name administrative centralization. ... in the United States administrative centralization does not exist. ...But in the United States governmental centralization exists to the highest point." Alexis de Tocqueville, *Democracy in America*, Vol. 1, Part 1, Ch. 5. Tocqueville, of course, observed our Republic prior to its vast increase in administrative centralization in the 20th century.

26 "A central power, however enlightened, however learned one imagines it, cannot gather to itself alone all the details of the life of a great people. It cannot do it because such a work exceeds human strength." Alexis de Tocqueville, *Democracy in America*, Vol. 1, Part 1, Ch. 5.

27 "In a large republic, the common good is sacrificed to a thousand considerations; it is subordinated to exceptions; it depends upon accidents. In a small one, the public good is better felt, better known, lies nearer to each citizen; abuses are less extensive there and consequently less protected." Montesquieu, *Spirit of the Laws*, Bk. 8, Ch. 16.

28 "If some abuses are introduced somewhere, they are corrected by the healthy parts." Montesquieu, *Spirit of the Laws*, Bk. 9, Ch. 1.

29 "...you [France] had all that combination, and all that opposition of interests, you had that action and counteraction which, in the natural and in the political world, from the reciprocal struggle of discordant powers,

draws out the harmony of the universe. These opposed and conflicting interests... interpose a salutary check to all precipitate resolutions; They render deliberation a matter not of choice, but of necessity; they make all change a subject of compromise, which naturally begets moderation; they produce temperaments, preventing the sore evil of harsh, crude, unqualified reformations; and rendering all the headlong exertions of arbitrary power, in the few or in the many, for ever impracticable." Edmund Burke, *Reflections on the Revolution in France*.

30 "One who might want to usurp could scarcely have equal credit in all the federated states." Montesquieu, *Spirit of the Laws*, Bk. 9, Ch. 1.

31 "In a single republic, all the power surrendered by the people, is submitted to the administration of a single government; and usurpations are guarded against by a division of the government into distinct and separate departments. In the compound republic of America, the power surrendered by the people, is first divided between two distinct governments, and then the portion allotted to each, subdivided among distinct and separate departments. Hence a double security arises to the rights of the people. The different governments will controul each other; at the same time that each will be controuled by itself." James Madison, *Federalist No. 51*.

32 The 2nd Amendment invokes "a well-regulated militia," implying that firearm regulation short of prohibition is constitutional; Congress and the States share responsibility for governing the militia, but the other uses of arms such as hunting or self-defense mostly fall under the powers reserved to the States to govern. *Roe v. Wade* forbids States from outlawing abortion, but allows them to regulate it. Some citizens consider abortion murder, and so believe that precedent erroneous; but laws concerning murder, too, are passed by the States, and their violation is tried in state courts. Federal jurisdiction is limited to certain crimes: see Art. 1, Sec. 8 and Art 2, Sec 2-3 of the *U.S. Constitution*.

33 See *Federalist No. 44*, in which James Madison defends the Necessary and Proper Clause.

34 Yet as noted previously, the best method of reducing bureaucracy in most cases is to increase discretion, which is most effectively done by allowing lower levels of government to exercise the powers reserved to them.

35 "Prior to the rebellion, by common consent, the right to enslave as well

as to disfranchise both native and foreign-born citizens, was conceded to the states. But the one grand principle, settled by the war and the reconstruction legislation, is the supremacy of national power to protect the citizens of the United States in their right to freedom and the elective franchise, against any and every interference on the part of the several states. And again and again, have the American people asserted the triumph of this principle, by their own overwhelming majorities for Lincoln and Grant. The one issue of the last two presidential elections was, whether the 14th and 15th amendments should be considered the irrevocable will of the people; and the decision was, they shall be – and that it is not only the right, but the duty of the national government to protect all United States citizens in the full enjoyment and free exercise of all their privileges and immunities against any attempt of any state to deny or abridge." Susan B. Anthony, "Is It a Crime for a U.S. Citizen to Vote?" speech, April 3, 1873.

36 "But I think that administrative centralization is fit only to enervate the peoples who submit to it, because it constantly tends to diminish the spirit of the city in them. Administrative centralization, it is true, succeeds in uniting at a given period and in a certain place all the disposable strengths of the nation, but it is harmful to the reproduction of strength. It makes the nation triumph on the day of combat and diminishes its power in the long term. It can therefore contribute admirably to the passing greatness of one man, not to the lasting prosperity of a people." Alexis de Tocqueville, *Democracy in America*, Vol. 1, Part 1, Ch. 5. We speak of economic and regulatory affairs; Lincoln's successors after Grant were grievously wrong to abdicate the upkeep of civil rights, which also weakened the Union.

NO. 3 – ON REPRESENTATIVE GOVERNMENT

37 "Men of factious tempers, of local prejudices, or of sinister designs, may by intrigue, by corruption or by other means, first obtain the suffrages, and then betray the interests of the people." James Madison, *Federalist No. 10*.

38 Opinion polls, if premature and hasty, turn democracy into a hall of mirrors. Mice are made into giants, for an aura of victory envelops those who lead early, though the poll is taken from a small sample of voters not yet familiar with any candidate; likewise are giants reduced to mice. Endless polls also sap representatives' will to use their judgment,

for which the people elected them. They follow the polls, chasing an illusion of the people's wishes; but the people often are not yet decided. The people meant to elect a leader; instead they install an aimless and inconstant follower.

39 The 24-hour news and social media have reduced the world's intricacies to sound-bites, which lull the people into false understanding; they also nationalize every local issue, eroding the federal system by leading citizens to believe that something that has happened in New York must also affect them in Texas, when often this is not the case.

40 "However deceived in generalities, men are not deceived in particulars." Niccolò Machiavelli, *Discourses on Titus Livy*, Bk. 1, Ch. 47.

41 As goes the saying famously attributed to Abraham Lincoln: "You can fool all of the people some of the time and some of the people all of the time, but you cannot fool all of the people all of the time."

42 "If we take into account the momentary humors or dispositions which may happen to prevail in particular parts of the society, and to which a wise administration will never be inattentive, is the man whose situation leads to extensive inquiry and information less likely to be a competent judge of their nature, extent and foundation than one whose observation does not travel beyond the circle of his neighbors and acquaintances?" Alexander Hamilton, *Federalist No. 35*.

43 "But to form a free government; that is, to temper together those opposite elements of liberty and restraint in one consistent work, requires much thought, deep reflection, a sagacious, powerful, and combining mind." Edmund Burke, *Reflections on the Revolution in France*.

44 A confederated government draws its authority only from the governments of its various parts, and a centralized government only directly from the whole body of the people.

45 "The House of Representatives will derive its powers from the people of America, and the people will be represented in the same proportion, and on the same principle, as they are in the Legislature of a particular State. So far the Government is national, not federal. The Senate on the other hand will derive its powers from the States, as political and co-equal societies; and these will be represented on the principle of equality in the Senate, as they now are in the existing Congress. So far the government is federal, not national. The executive power will be derived from a very compound source. The immediate election of the

President is to be made by the States in their political characters. The votes allotted to them, are in a compound ratio, which considers them partly as distinct and co-equal societies; partly as unequal members of the same society. ...From this aspect of the Government, it appears to be of a mixed character presenting at least as many federal as national features." James Madison, *Federalist No. 39*.

46 California being a notorious example, but this addiction surfaces in states as different as Maryland and Oklahoma.

47 Referendums are more appropriate at lower levels of government: of some use for a city, more for a town, and much for a neighborhood, as the people are familiar with the issue being decided and the effects of their decision.

48 Though, since it is the nature of such things to lurk unseen, to precisely measure lobbying's effect is impossible.

49 "It is equally unnecessary to dilate on the appointment of senators by the state legislatures. Among the various modes which might have been devised for constituting this branch of the government, that which has been proposed by the convention is probably the most congenial with public opinion. It is recommended by the double advantage of favoring a select appointment, and of giving to the state governments such an agency in the formation of the federal government, as must secure the authority of the former; and may form a convenient link between the two systems." James Madison, *Federalist No. 62*.

50 "...there are particular moments in public affairs, when the people stimulated by some irregular passion... may call for measures which they themselves will afterwards be the most ready to lament and condemn. In these critical moments, how salutary will be the interference of some temperate and respectable body of citizens, in order to check the misguided career, and to suspend the blow meditated by the people against themselves, until reason, justice and truth, can regain their authority over the public mind?" James Madison, *Federalist No. 62*.

51 "But when the leaders choose to make themselves bidders at an auction of popularity, their talents, in the construction of the state, will be of no service. They will become flatterers instead of legislators; the instruments, not the guides of the people." Edmund Burke, *Reflections on the Revolution in France*.

52 "The federal constitution made the two chambers come from the votes of

the people as well; but it varied the conditions of eligibility and the mode of election, so that if one of the two branches of the legislature did not represent different interests from the other, as in certain nations, it at least represented a superior wisdom." Alexis de Tocqueville, *Democracy in America*, Vol. 1, Part 1, Ch. 8.

53 Per judicial precedent, for good reason: the continual recall of Senators would severely disrupt federal legislation.

54 Unaffiliated legislators could together nominate an independent candidate, or instead vote with one of the parties.

55 "…the principle of democracy is corrupted not only when the spirit of equality is lost but also when the spirit of extreme equality is taken up and each one wants to be the equal of those chosen to command. So the people, finding intolerable even the power which they entrust to the others, want to do everything themselves: to deliberate for the senate, to execute for the magistrates, and to cast aside all the judges." Montesquieu, *Spirit of the Laws*, Bk. 8, Ch. 2.

NO. 4 – ON BUREAUCRACY

56 "All legislative powers herein granted shall be vested in a Congress of the United States, which shall consist of a Senate and House of Representatives." *U.S. Constitution*, Art. 1, Sec. 1; "No Money shall be drawn from the Treasury, but in Consequence of Appropriations made by Law;" Art. 1, Sec. 9.

57 "The constitution of the legislative is the first and fundamental act of society, whereby provision is made for the continuance of their union, under the direction of persons, and bonds of laws, made by persons authorized thereunto, by the consent and appointment of the people, without which no one man, or number of men, amongst them, can have authority of making laws that shall be binding to the rest." John Locke, *Second Treatise of Government*, Ch. 19, Para. 212.

58 "When any one, or more, shall take upon them to make laws, whom the people have not appointed to do so, they make laws without authority, which the people are not therefore bound to obey… when other laws are set up, and other rules pretended, and inforced, then what the legislative, constituted by the society, have enacted, it is plain that the legislative is changed. Whoever introduces new laws, not being thereunto authorized by the fundamental appointment of the society, or subverts the old, disowns and overturns the power by which they were made, and so sets

up a new [and illegitimate] legislative." John Locke, *Second Treatise of Government*, Ch. 19, Para. 212 and 214.

59 "Another effect of public instability is the unreasonable advantage it gives to the sagacious, the enterprising and the moneyed few, over the industrous and uninformed mass of the people. Every new regulation concerning commerce or revenue, or in any manner affecting the value of the different species of property, presents a new harvest to those who watch the change, and can trace its consequences; a harvest reared not by themselves but by the toils and cares of the great body of their fellow citizens. This is a state of things in which it may be said with some truth that laws are made for the few not for the many." James Madison, *Federalist No. 62*.

60 "Regulatory action shall not be undertaken unless the potential benefits to society for the regulation outweigh the potential costs to society." Executive Order 12291, issued by President Ronald Reagan, Feb. 1981.

61 "If you examine the formalities of justice in relation to the difficulties a citizen endures to have his goods returned to him or to obtain satisfaction for some insult, you will doubtless find the formalities too many; if you consider them in relation to the liberty and security of the citizens, you will often find them too few, and you will see that the penalties, expenses, delays, and even the dangers of justice are the price each citizen pays for his liberty." Montesquieu, *Spirit of the Laws*, Bk. 6, Ch. 2.

62 Article 1, Section 8 grants Congress explicit power to define as crimes only "Piracies and Felonies committed on the high Seas, and Offenses against the Law of Nations." It also grants power to punish counterfeiting. Article 3 adds power to punish treason, and restricts to seven categories those cases which may be tried by the federal courts.

63 "Centralization succeeds without difficulty in impressing a regular style on current affairs; in skillfully regimenting the details of social orderliness; in repressing slight disorders and small offenses; in maintaining society in a status quo that is properly neither decadence nor progress; in keeping in the social body a sort of administrative somnolence that administrators are accustomed to calling good order and public tranquility. It excels, in a word, at preventing, not doing." Alexis de Tocqueville, *Democracy in America*, Vol. 1, Part 1, Ch. 5.

64 "UK Government – Did we rule the Empire with 4,000 civil servants?"

UK National Archives Blog, Aug 1, 2012. The author debunks the claim that the Empire was administered by only 4,000 civil servants, but notes that most of the imperial administration was done in a decentralized manner. His high-end estimate of 40,000 civil servants in Britain pales in comparison to the two million employed by the federal government of the United States in 2015. See "Sizing Up the Executive Branch: Fiscal Year 2015," U.S. Office of Personnel Management, published June 2016.

65 The "make one, scrap two" rule introduced by the present administration deserves credit here.

66 Excluding the Vice President.

67 For instance, the Department of Transportation could be accountable to the Department of the Interior.

68 So long as Congress does not abdicate a general power enumerated to the federal government by the Constitution.

69 We refer here to true judicial courts, empowered under Article 3 of the Constitution, rather than expanding the quasi-judicial "Article 2" courts which adjudicate regulation under the aegis of the executive branch.

70 "[The judiciary] may truly be said to have neither Force nor Will, but merely judgment… The courts must declare the sense of the law; and if they should be disposed to exercise Will instead of Judgment, the consequence would equally be the substitution of their pleasure to that of the legislative body." Alexander Hamilton, *Federalist No. 78.*

71 "If the judge had been able to attack laws in a theoretical and general manner, if he had been able to take the initiative and censure the legislator, he would have entered onto the political stage with a bang; having become the champion or adversary of one party, he would have appealed to all the passions that divide the country to take part in the conflict." Alexis de Tocqueville, *Democracy in America*, Vol. 1, Part 1, Ch. 6. His description sounds prophetic.

72 "I recommend that a law be enacted to regulate interstate commerce in misbranded and adulterated foods, drinks, and drugs. Such law would protect legitimate manufacture and commerce, and would tend to secure the health and welfare of the consuming public." Theodore Roosevelt, *Fifth Message to Congress*, Dec. 5, 1905.

73 The text of the clause is as follows: "The Congress shall have Power… To regulate commerce with foreign Nations, and among the several States and with the Indian Tribes;" *U.S. Constitution*, Art. 1, Sec. 8.

74 As court precedent held before 1942. Before, peoples and goods in commerce, instrumentalities of commerce, and channels of commerce could be regulated. Later, particularly after the *Wickard v. Filburn* case in 1942, the standard expanded to peoples and things having a substantial effect on commerce, which opened the door to excess.

NO. 5 – ON THE NATIONAL DEBT

75 Whereas the 'deficit' refers to the amount the government borrows in a single year; i.e., the shortfall between that year's budget and government revenue. The public (or national) debt refers to the sum total of money that the government owes, accumulated over the course of many years of deficits, and incorporating interest.

76 "To relieve the present exigency is always the object which principally interests those immediately concerned in the administration of public affairs. The future liberation of the public revenue, they leave to the care of posterity." Adam Smith, *The Wealth of Nations*, Bk. 5, Ch. 3.

77 "That exigencies are to be expected to occur, in the affairs of nations, in which there will be a necessity for borrowing. That loans in times of public danger, especially from foreign war, are found an indispensable resource, even to the wealthiest of them." Alexander Hamilton, *First Report on Public Credit*.

78 10-year U.S. Treasury bond yields have in the past decade averaged between 2-3%, less, in fact, than the decades preceding it; this represents the confidence the world reposes in the full faith and credit of the U.S. government. The data may be found on the Treasury's website, under "Daily Treasury Long Term Rate Data" in its Resource Center.

79 The same logic, of course, applies to the domestic portion of the debt; domestic bondholders, by virtue of residing in the United States, mostly hold their wealth in dollars and thus would be similarly averse to devaluation.

80 "When funding [of debt], besides, has made a certain progress, the multiplication of taxes which it brings along with it sometimes impairs as much the ability of private people to accumulate even in time of peace, as the other system [of saving] would in time of war." Adam Smith, *The Wealth of Nations*, Bk. 5, Ch. 3.

81 Given that tax rates are proportional to income and profit; a strong economy brings higher incomes and profits, and thus more tax revenue,

even when the tax rate remains constant.

82 "In Great Britain, from the time that we had first recourse to the ruinous expedient of perpetual funding, the reduction of the public debt in time of peace, has never borne any proportion to its accumulation in time of war." Adam Smith, *The Wealth of Nations*, Bk. 5, Ch. 3.

83 Great consideration must be given to national independence movements which broke apart the British Empire; the United States, fortunately, faces no such risk to its territorial integrity today. Britain also suffered extensive physical damage during the world wars – a risk, which, if it finds itself in a major war, our Republic could also be exposed to.

84 "Great Britain seems to support with ease, a burden which, half a century ago, nobody believed her capable of supporting. Let us not, however, upon this account rashly conclude that she is capable of supporting any burden; nor even be too confident that she could support, without great distress, a burden a little greater than what has already been laid upon her." Adam Smith, *The Wealth of Nations*, Bk. 5, Ch. 3.

85 Common estimates predict that China's nominal gross domestic product (GDP) will overtake that of the United States in the 2030s. Others contend that, as China's purchasing power parity (PPP) is now higher than the United States', that China is already the world's largest economy. There is not, however, full agreement on the subject.

86 "That liberation [of public funds], it is evident, can never be brought about without either some very considerable augmentation of the public revenue, or some equally considerable reduction of the public expence." Adam Smith, *The Wealth of Nations*, Bk. 5, Ch. 3.

87 For instance, as the future budgets of military units are cut if they do not spend the entirety of their present budget, units have every incentive to embark upon a wasteful spending spree at the end of each fiscal year, and no incentive to conserve public funds. It is unsurprising, therefore, that the DoD recently failed its first full audit since 1991; and it is also unsurprising, but greatly disheartening, that its public reaction to that event bordered upon apathy. "We failed the audit, but we never expected to pass it," said the Deputy Secretary of Defense at the time, according to a news article on the subject. "Pentagon Fails Its First-Ever Audit, Official Says," *Reuters*, Nov. 15, 2018.

88 "While the Navy is continuing to accept delivery of ships, it has received $24 billion more in funding than originally planned but has 50 fewer

ships in its inventory today, as compared to the goals it first established in its 2007 long-range shipbuilding plan." The Government Accountability Office, in a report titled "Navy Shipbuilding: Past Performance Provides Valuable Lessons for Future Investments," June 6, 2018.

89   "The third and last duty of the sovereign or commonwealth is that of erecting and maintaining those public institutions and those public works, which, though they may be in the highest degree advantageous to a great society, are, however, of such a nature, that the profit could never repay the expence to any individual or small number of individuals, and which it cannot therefore be expected that any individual or small number of individuals should erect or maintain." Adam Smith, *The Wealth of Nations*, Bk. 5, Ch. 1. The granting of patents, which is also a constitutional duty of the federal government, sometimes solves this problem for private firms by giving them a financial incentive to bear the costs of research. But there must nevertheless be some prospect of profit for a patent to work, and not all public goods are profitable. Governments may also help to fund long-term research which may someday be profitable, but is in too early of a stage for private firms to realize the profit within the time they have available to produce a return on investment.

NO. 6 – ON ENTITLEMENTS

90   Montesquieu saw this; Laffer formalized it. "…the lord and those who levy the revenues for the prince, each in his turn, will harass the [serf] and will, one after the other, collect from him until he perishes from poverty or flees into the woods." "Liberty has produced excessive taxes, but the effect of these excessive taxes is to produce servitude in their turn, and the effect of servitude is to produce a decrease in taxes." Montesquieu, *Spirit of the Laws*, Bk. 13, Ch. 5, 15.

91   This danger was a concern of the Anti-Federalists, including 'Brutus' quoted above, who objected to the power of the federal government to tax citizens directly. The Federalists refuted this charge, with good reason: the system of requisitions under the Articles of Confederation had failed then, and would fail again today. But the principle has nonetheless been shown to be valid since the introduction of the large federal programs of the 20th century.

92   As in the 18th-century proverb that "fire is a good servant but a cruel master." The use of that metaphor in relation to government has

been attributed to George Washington; whether or not he said it, the comparison is appropriate.

93 "Whosoever uses forces without right, as everyone does in society, who does it without law, puts himself into a state of war with those against whom he so uses it; and in that state all former ties are cancelled, all other rights cease, and everyone has a right to defend himself, and to resist the aggressor." John Locke, *Second Treatise of Government*, Ch. 19, Para. 232. As goes the Declaration of Independence: "When, in the Course of human events..."

94 *U.S. Constitution*, Article 4, Section 4.

95 "When, by different taxes upon the necessaries and conveniences of life, the owners and employers of capital stock find, that whatever revenue they derive from it, will not, in a particular country, purchase the same quantity of those necessaries and conveniences which an equal revenue would in almost any other, they will be disposed to remove to some other. And when, in order to raise those taxes, all or the greater part of merchants and manufacturers, that is, all or the greater part of employers of great capitals, come to be continually exposed to the mortifying and vexatious visits of the tax-gatherers, this disposition to remove will soon be changed into an actual removal." Adam Smith, *The Wealth of Nations*, Bk. 5, Ch. 3.

96 "The Secretary, after mature reflection on this point, entertains a full conviction, that an assumption of the debts of the particular states by the union, and a like provision for them, as for those of the union, will be a measure of sound policy and substantial justice." Alexander Hamilton, *First Report on Public Credit*. If the federal government may be liable to assume the States' debts, it is logical that it ought also to be empowered to set limits on them.

97 Vermont is the exception. As those statutes take different forms, and because costs are often difficult to predict, not all state budgets are balanced in the final reckoning. The attempt nonetheless produces results in the aggregate: the Census Bureau estimated, in its 2016 State & Local Government Finance Survey, that state debts combined were $3 trillion, roughly a sixth of the $20 trillion federal debt recorded by the Treasury Department at the time.

98 In essence, a furtherance of the existing system by which the States may avail themselves of additional federal funds for Medicaid. In our

envisioned reform, States would have a greater say in designing their Medicaid schemes.

99 I.e., a gentleman of sixty years of age at the time of this writing, who has paid tax for Social Security over the course of his working life and who is soon to retire, would still receive nearly the entire federal benefit as it now stands; a lady of forty would receive when she retires somewhat less in proportion of the federal benefit, and the remaining proportion in accordance with the plan of her State; and a boy of fourteen, who has not yet begun to work or pay tax, would receive upon his eventual retirement only that benefit which his State has determined.

100 "The Citizens of each State shall be entitled to all Privileges and Immunities of Citizens in the several States." *U.S. Constitution*, Article 4, Section 2.

101 This may be done by expanding the existing tax credit for moves, or by a more direct means.

102 "The particular policy of the national and of the State systems of finance might now and then not exactly coincide, and might require reciprocal forbearances." Alexander Hamilton, *Federalist No. 32*.

103 "The Secretary conceives, that it will be sound policy, to carry the duties upon articles of this kind [wines and distilled spirits], as high as will be consistent with the practicability of a safe collection. This will lessen the necessity, both of having recourse to direct taxation, and of accumulating duties where they would be more inconvenient to trade, and upon objects, which are more to be regarded as necessaries of life." Alexander Hamilton, *First Report on Public Credit*.

104 "As revenue is the essential engine by which the means of answering the national exigencies must be procured, the power of procuring that article in its full extent, must necessarily be comprehended in that of providing for those exigencies." Alexander Hamilton, *Federalist No. 31*.

105 "Taxes can be increased in most republics because the citizen, who believes he is paying to himself, has the will to pay them and ordinarily has the power to do so as a result of the nature of the government." Montesquieu, *Spirit of the Laws*, Bk.13, Ch. 13.

106 "Duties on commodities are the ones the least felt by the people, because no formal request is made for them." Montesquieu, *Spirit of the Laws*, Bk. 13, Ch. 7.

107 "Taxes upon such consumable goods as are articles of luxury, are all

finally paid by the consumer, and generally in a manner that is very convenient for him. He pays them by little and little, as he has occasion to buy the goods. As he is at liberty too, either to buy, or not to buy, as he pleases, it must be his own fault if he ever suffers any considerable inconveniency from such taxes." Adam Smith, *The Wealth of Nations*, Bk. 5, Ch. 2.

NO. 7 – ON ECONOMIC INEQUALITY

108 A term used by economist Paul Krugman to describe the growth of income inequality in the U.S. since the 1970s.

109 "Probably the greatest harm done by vast wealth is the harm that we of moderate means do ourselves when we let the vices of envy and hatred enter deep into our own hearts." Theodore Roosevelt, "Trust Speech," Aug. 23, 1902.

110 "There is a manly and legitimate passion for equality that incites men to want all to be strong and esteemed. This passion tends to elevate the small to the rank of the great; but one also encounters a depraved taste for equality in the human heart that brings the weak to want to draw the strong to their level and that reduces men to preferring equality in servitude to inequality in freedom." Alexis de Tocqueville, *Democracy in America*, Vol. 1, Part 1, Ch. 3.

111 "Tolerate neither rich men nor beggars. These two estates, which are naturally inseparable, are equally fatal to the common good. From the one come the fomenters of tyranny, and from the other the tyrants. It is always between them that public liberty becomes a matter of commerce. The one buys it and the other sells it." Jean-Jacques Rousseau, *On the Social Contract*, Bk. 2, Ch. 11.

112 "…where the competition is free, the rivalship of competitors, who are all endeavouring to jostle one another out of employment, obliges every man to endeavor to execute his work with a certain degree of exactness. …Rivalship and emulation render excellency, even in mean professions, an object of ambition, and frequently occasion the very greatest exertions." Adam Smith, *The Wealth of Nations*, Bk. 5, Ch. 1.

113 "We still continue in a period of unbounded prosperity. This prosperity is not the creature of the law, but undoubtedly the laws under which we work have been instrumental in creating the conditions which made it possible, and by unwise legislation it would be easy enough to destroy it." Theodore Roosevelt, *Second Message to Congress*, Dec. 2, 1902.

114 "The Congress shall have Power… to establish uniform Laws on the subject of Bankruptcies… to promote the Progress of Science and useful Arts, by securing for limited Times to Authors and Inventors the exclusive Right to their respective Writings and Discoveries…" *U.S. Constitution*, Art. 1, Sec. 8; "No State shall… pass any Law impairing the Obligation of Contracts…" Art. 1, Sec. 10.

115 "By a perpetual monopoly, all the other subjects of the state are taxed very absurdly in two different ways; first, by the high price of goods, which, in the case of a free trade, they could buy much cheaper; and secondly, by their total exclusion from a branch of business, which it might be both convenient and profitable for many of them to carry on. It is for the most worthless of all purposes too that they are taxed in this manner. It is merely to enable the company to support the negligence, profusion, and malversation of their own servants, whose disorderly conduct seldom allows the dividend of the company to exceed the ordinary rate of profit in trades which are altogether free, and very frequently makes it fall even a good deal short of that rate." Adam Smith, *The Wealth of Nations*, Bk. 5, Ch. 1.

116 As it did, effectively, in the crisis of 2008.

117 "Though the principles of the banking trade may appear somewhat abstruse, the practice is capable of being reduced to strict rules. To depart on any occasion from those rules, in consequence of some flattering speculation of extraordinary gain, is almost always extremely dangerous, and frequently fatal to the banking company which attempts it." Adam Smith, *The Wealth of Nations*, Bk. 5, Ch. 1.

118 "There will undoubtedly be periods of depression. The wave will recede; but the tide will advance. This Nation is seated on a continent flanked by two great oceans. It is composed of men the descendants of pioneers, or, in a sense, pioneers themselves; of men winnowed out from among the nations of the Old World by the energy, boldness, and love of adventure found in their own eager hearts. Such a Nation, so placed, will surely wrest success from fortune." Theodore Roosevelt, *Second Message to Congress*, Dec. 2, 1902.

119 Thoughtful proposals have been made by the *Economist* newspaper, and others, on antitrust policy regarding data.

120 Several state governments have already taken the initiative in this regard; they ought to press it.

121 The scorpion asks the frog to carry it across a river; the frog accepts, because it knows that if the scorpion stings it while crossing, both will drown; but the scorpion stings regardless. It says, "I cannot help it. It is in my nature."

122 This does not imply a monopoly on weapon ownership, protected by the 2nd Amendment. The right of private citizens to bear arms guards liberty; the ability of firms to use arms against citizens, or foreigners, is a menace to it.

123 "In other universities the teacher is prohibited from receiving any honorary or fee from his pupils, and his salary constitutes the whole of the revenue which he derives from his office. His interest is, in this case, set as directly in opposition to his duty as it is possible to set it. It is in the interest of every man to live as much at his ease as he can; and if his emoluments are to be precisely the same, whether he does, or does not perform some very laborious duty, it is certainly his interest, at least as interest is vulgarly understood, either to neglect it altogether, or, if he is subject to some authority which will not suffer him to do this, to perform it in as careless and slovenly a manner as that authority will permit." Adam Smith, *The Wealth of Nations*, Bk. 5, Ch. 1.

124 Currently, a high school diploma in one State does not necessarily reflect the same standard of education as one in another. Firms must guess which States provide better-educated workers, and some discriminate: a promising hire may be overlooked because their State has a lower standard of education. A federal exam would dispel this fog.

125 The technical definition of monopoly being a market in which there is only one seller.

126 With, as noted in our previous essay, federal support to States with less capacity to afford necessary investments.

127 Massachusetts did so in 2006, with a reasonable measure of success.

NO. 8 – ON TRADE

128 "If instead of a farmer and artificer, there were a farmer only, he would be under the necessity of devoting a part of his labour to the fabrication of clothing and other articles, which he would procure of the artificer, in the case of there being such a person; and of course he would be able to devote less labor to the cultivation of his farm; and would draw from it a proportionally less product." Alexander Hamilton, *Report on the Subject*

of Manufactures, Dec 5, 1791.

129 "By opening a new and inexhaustible market to all the commodities of Europe, it [the discovery of America] gave occasion to new divisions of labour and improvements of art, which, in the narrow circle of the ancient commerce, could never have taken place for want of a market to take off the greater part of their produce." Adam Smith, *The Wealth of Nations*, Bk. 4, Ch. 1.

130 "Sir, those who contend for the removal of impediments upon the import of a great article of subsistence, such as corn, start with an immense advantage in the argument. The natural presumption is in favour of free and unrestricted importation." Sir Robert Peel, speech to Parliament on the Repeal of the Corn Laws, Jan 22, 1846.

131 "It has justly been observed, that there is scarcely any thing of greater moment to the economy of a nation, than the proper division of labor. The separation of occupations causes each to be carried to a much greater perfection, than it could possibly acquire, if they were blended... The greater skill and dexterity naturally resulting from a constant and undivided attention to a single object... The economy of time – by avoiding the loss of it, incident to a frequent transition from one operation to another of a different nature." Alexander Hamilton, *Report on Manufactures*.

132 "I have heard them called protections; but taxes they are, and taxes they shall be in my mouth, as long as I have the honor of a seat in this House. The bread-tax is a tax primarily levied upon the poorer classes; it is a tax, at the lowest estimate, of 40 per cent above the price we should pay if there were a free trade in corn." Richard Cobden, speech to Parliament, Aug 25, 1841.

133 "The natural effect of commerce is to lead to peace. Two nations that trade with each other become reciprocally dependent; if one has an interest in buying, the other has an interest in selling, and all unions are founded on mutual needs." Montesquieu, *Spirit of the Laws*, Bk. 20, Ch. 2.

134 "Nothing, however, can be more absurd than this whole doctrine of the balance of trade, upon which, not only these restraints, but almost all regulations of commerce are founded. When two places trade with one another, this doctrine supposes that, if the balance be even, neither of them either loses or gains; but if it leans in any degree to one

side, that one of them loses, and the other gains in proportion to its declension from the exact equilibrium. Both suppositions are false. A trade which is forced by means of bounties and monopolies, may be, and commonly is disadvantageous to the country in whose favor it is meant to be established... But that trade which, without force or constraint, is naturally and regularly carried on between any two places, is always advantageous, though not always equally so, to both." Adam Smith, *The Wealth of Nations*, Bk. 4, Ch. 2.

135 "It seems not always to be recollected, that nations, who have neither mines nor manufactures, can only obtain the manufactured articles, of which they stand in need, by an exchange of the products of their soils; and that, if those who can best furnish them with such articles are unwilling to give a due course to this exchange, they must of necessity make every possible effort to manufacture for themselves, the effect of which is that the manufacturing nations abridge the natural advantages of their situation, through an unwillingness to permit the Agricultural countries to enjoy the advantages of theirs, and sacrifice the interests of a mutually beneficial intercourse to the vain project of selling everything and buying nothing." Alexander Hamilton, *Report on Manufactures*.

136 "By means of such regulations, indeed, a particular manufacture may sometimes be acquired sooner than it could have been otherwise, and after a certain time may be made at home as cheap or cheaper than in a foreign country. But though the industry of the society may be thus carried with advantage into a particular channel sooner than it could have been otherwise, it will by no means follow that the sum total, either of its industry, or of its revenue, can ever be augmented by any such regulation." Adam Smith, *The Wealth of Nations*, Bk. 4, Ch. 2.

137 Since 1990, the proportion of world trade across the Pacific has held generally steady, but that across the Atlantic has fallen whereas that across the Eurasian landmass has risen, placing China increasingly at the world's economic center. Statistics made public by the World Trade Organization in its 2013 World Trade Report show this shift.

138 "No goods are sent abroad but those for which the demand is supposed to be greater abroad than at home, and of which the returns consequently, it is expected, will be of more value at home than the commodities exported." Adam Smith, *The Wealth of Nations*, Bk. 4, Ch. 2.

139 "That it was the spirit of monopoly which originally both invented and propagated this doctrine, cannot be doubted; and they who first taught

it were by no means such fools as they who believed it. In every country it always is and must be the interest of the great body of the people to buy whatever they want of those who sell it cheapest." Adam Smith, *The Wealth of Nations*, Bk. 4, Ch. 2.

140 "Home is in this manner the center, if I may say so, round which the capitals of the inhabitants of every country are continually circulating, and towards which they are always tending, though by particular causes they may sometimes be driven off and repelled from it towards more distant employments." Adam Smith, *The Wealth of Nations*, Bk. 4, Ch. 2.

141 "If there be anything in a remark often to be met with – namely that there is, in the genius of the people of this country, a peculiar aptitude for mechanic improvements…" Alexander Hamilton, *Report on Manufactures*.

142 Such as the requirement for a proportion of automobiles to be manufactured by workers earning $16 an hour, which is a disguised tariff to move production from Mexico. A few U.S. citizens benefit from it; more suffer by it.

143 This Republic has been struck from that quarter before, on December the 7th of 1941.

144 "There may be good policy in retaliations of this kind, when there is a probability that they will procure the repeal of the high duties or prohibitions complained of. The recovery of a great foreign market will generally more than compensate the transitory inconveniency of paying dearer during a short time for some sorts of goods. …When there is no probability that any such repeal can be procured, it seems a bad method of compensating the injury done to certain classes of our people, to do another injury ourselves, not only to those classes, but to almost all other classes of them." Adam Smith, *The Wealth of Nations*, Bk. 4, Ch. 2.

145 Some community colleges have already begun to do so; their States ought to support and expand these efforts.

146 "Let the same natural liberty of exercising what species of industry they please, be restored to all his majesty's subjects, in the same manner as to soldiers and seamen; that is, break down the exclusive privileges of corporations, and repeal the statute of apprenticeship, both which are real encroachments upon natural liberty, and add to these the repeal of the law of settlements, so that a poor workman, when thrown out of employment either in one trade or in one place, may seek for it in

another trade or another place, without the fear either of a prosecution or of a removal, and neither the public nor the individuals will suffer much more from the occasional disbanding some particular class of manufactures, than from that of soldiers." Adam Smith, *The Wealth of Nations*, Bk. 4, Ch. 2.

147 "The case in which it may sometimes be a matter of deliberation, how far, or in what manner, it is proper to restore the free importation of foreign goods, after it has been for some time interrupted, is, when particular manufactures, by means of high duties of prohibitions upon all foreign goods which can come into competition with them, have been so far extended as to employ a great multitude of hands. Humanity may in this case require that the freedom of trade should be restored only by slow gradations, and with a good deal of reserve and circumspection." Adam Smith, *The Wealth of Nations*, Bk. 4, Ch. 2.

148 "There seem, however, to be two cases in which it will generally be advantageous to lay some burden upon foreign, for the encouragement of domestic industry. The first is, when some particular sort of industry is necessary for the defence of the country." Adam Smith, *The Wealth of Nations*, Bk. 4, Ch. 2.

149 Canada principally comes to mind, as do Western Europe and Japan so long as maritime passage to them is likely to remain uncontested. It does us no good that an ally is stalwart if we may be cut off from them.

NO. 9 – ON CITIZENSHIP

150 "The question with me is not whether you have a right to render your people miserable, but whether it is not your interest to make them happy?" Edmund Burke, speech to Parliament on Conciliation with America, Mar. 22, 1775.

151 One effective means of encouragement is the Child Tax Credit, which ought to be upheld and perhaps expanded.

152 "Recognize the fact that the rights of the humblest citizen are as worthy of protection as are those of the highest, and your problem will be solved; and, whatever may be in store for it in the future, whether prosperity, or adversity; whether it shall have foes without, or foes within, whether there shall be peace, or war; based upon the eternal principles of truth, justice and humanity, and with no class having any cause of complaint or grievance, your Republic will stand and flourish forever." Frederick Douglass, "Lessons of the Hour" speech, Jan. 9, 1894.

153 "...since all things of men are in motion and cannot stay steady, they must either rise or fall; and to many things that reason does not bring you, necessity brings you. [Thus] in ordering a republic there is need… to order it so that if indeed necessity brings it to expand, it can conserve what it has seized." Niccolò Machiavelli, *Discourses on Titus Livy*, Bk. 1, Ch. 6.

154 "...the government of a conqueror, imposed by force on the subdued, against whom he had no right of war, or who joined not in the war against him, where he had right, has no obligation upon them." John Locke, *Second Treatise of Government*, Ch. 16, Para. 187.

155 Except Canada, Australia, and New Zealand, which, because they were given some representation, remain closer to Britain than other former parts of the Empire; and Scotland, Wales, and Northern Ireland, which, because they were given full representation, remain part of the United Kingdom to this day.

156 "First, Sir, permit me to observe, that the use of force alone is but temporary. It may subdue for a moment; but it does not remove the necessity of subduing again: and a nation is not governed, which is perpetually to be conquered." Edmund Burke, speech to Parliament on Conciliation with America, Mar. 22, 1775.

157 "My idea therefore, without considering whether we yield as a matter of right, or grant as a matter of favour, is to admit the people of our Colonies into an interest in the constitution; and, by recording that admission in the Journals of Parliament, to give them as strong an assurance as the nature of the thing will admit, that we mean for ever to adhere to that solemn declaration of systematic indulgence." Burke, speech to Parliament on Conciliation with America, Mar. 22, 1775.

158 "Whatsoever cannot but be acknowledged to be of advantage to the society, and people in general, upon just and lasting measures, will always, when done, justify itself; and whenever the people shall chuse their representatives upon just and undeniably equal measures, suitable to the original frame of the government, it cannot be doubted to be the will and act of the society, whoever permitted or caused them so to do." John Locke, *Second Treatise of Government*, Ch. 13, Para. 158.

159 American Samoa has an even more unusual arrangement: its residents do not obtain U.S. citizenship by birth. Yet they have the highest rate of enlistment in the U.S. military; their commitment to the Union thus

cannot be doubted.

160 "It may well be doubted whether those tribes which reside within the acknowledged boundaries of the United States can, with strict accuracy, be denominated foreign nations. They may more correctly, perhaps, be denominated domestic dependent nations." Chief Justice John Marshall, written opinion in *Cherokee Nation v. Georgia*, 1831.

161 "Be it enacted by the Senate and House of Representatives of the United States of America in Congress assembled, that all non-citizen Indians born within the territorial limits of the United States be, and they are hereby, declared to be citizens of the United States." Indian Citizenship Act of 1924.

162 As the right to vote is assured to all U.S. citizens by the 15th Amendment and the Voting Rights Act of 1965.

163 "In general it may be remarked on this subject, that no political problem is less susceptible of a precise solution, than that which relates to the number most convenient for a representative legislature. ...Sixty or seventy men, may be more properly trusted with a given degree of power than six or seven. But it does not follow, that six or seven hundred would be proportionally a better depository. And if we carry on the supposition to six or seven thousand, the whole reasoning ought to be reversed. The truth is, that in all cases a certain number at least seems to be necessary to secure the benefits of free consultation and discussion, and to guard against too easy a combination for improper purposes: as on the other hand, the number ought at most to be kept within a certain limit, in order to avoid the confusion and intemperance of a multitude." James Madison, *Federalist No. 55*. The addition of a new State, the population of which is roughly one-third that of the now-smallest State, would require a tripling of the total number of Representatives – to 1305 – to remain in its current proportion. Yet, as we address below, the House is already in need of enlargement to restore proper proportion to the existing States. Doing both together would increase its size to nearly two thousand members. If we now lament deadlock in a chamber of 435, imagine the result at that size.

164 The population figures from the 2010 Census would suggest a seven-member delegation, wherein Guam would have three members, the Virgin Islands two members, and the Mariana Islands and American Samoa one member each.

165 "The District constituting the seat of Government of the United States shall appoint in such manner as the Congress may direct: A number of electors of President and Vice President equal to the whole number of Senators and Representatives in Congress to which the District would be entitled if it were a State, but in no event more than the least populous State; they shall be in addition to those appointed by the States, but they shall be considered, for the purposes of the election of President and Vice President, to be electors appointed by a State; and they shall meet in the District and perform such duties as provided by the twelfth article of amendment." 23rd Amendment to the *U.S. Constitution*.

166 Those States allocate some of their votes to the winning candidate in each of their Congressional districts, while reserving others to the winning candidate in the State at large.

167 The *New York Times*, in a two-part editorial entitled "America Needs a Bigger House," published Nov. 9, 2018.

168 "The proposition to disfranchise the colored voter of the South in order to solve the race problem I hereby denounce as a mean and cowardly proposition, utterly unworthy of an honest, truthful and grateful nation. It is a proposition to sacrifice friends in order to conciliate enemies, to surrender the constitution to the late rebels for the lack of moral courage to execute its provisions." Frederick Douglass, "Lessons of the Hour" speech, Jan. 9, 1894.

169 "All persons born or naturalized in the United States and subject to the jurisdiction thereof, are citizens of the United States and of the State wherein they reside. No State shall make or enforce any law which shall abridge the privileges or immunities of citizens of the United States; nor shall any State deprive any person of life, liberty, or property, without due process of law; nor deny to any person within its jurisdiction the equal protection of the laws." 14th Amendment to the *U.S. Constitution*.

170 "In old times when it was asked, 'How can we abolish slavery?' the answer was 'Quit stealing.' The same is the solution of the Race problem to-day. The whole thing can be done by simply no longer violating the amendments of the Constitution of the United States, and no longer evading the claims of justice. If this were done, there would be no negro problem to vex the South, or to vex the nation. Let the organic law of the land be honestly sustained and obeyed." Frederick Douglass, "Lessons of the Hour" speech, Jan. 9, 1894.

171 New Mexico, Arizona, California, Nevada, Utah, and Colorado.

NO. 10 – ON IMMIGRATION

172 "We are now a mighty nation; we are about thirty millions of people, and we own and inhabit about one-fifteenth part of the dry land of the whole earth. We run our memory back over the pages of history for about eighty-two years and we discover that we were then a very small people in point of numbers, vastly inferior to what we are now, with a vastly less extent of country, with vastly less of everything we deem desirable among men; we look upon that change as exceedingly advantageous to us and to our prosperity, and we fix upon something that happened away back, as in some way or other being connected with this rise of prosperity." Abraham Lincoln, speech in Chicago, Jul. 10, 1858.

173 "A man wrote me and said: 'You can go to live in France, but you cannot become a Frenchman. You can go to live in Germany or Turkey or Japan, but you cannot become a German, a Turk, or a Japanese. But anyone, from any corner of the Earth, can come to live in America and become an American.' …This, I believe, is one of the most important sources of America's greatness. We lead the world because, unique among nations, we draw our people – our strength – from every country and every corner of the world." Ronald Reagan, remarks at the Presentation of the Presidential Medal of Freedom, Jan. 19, 1989.

174 "We have besides these men descended by blood from our ancestors, among us perhaps half our people who are not descendants at all of these men; they are men who have come from Europe themselves, or whose ancestors have come hither and settled here, finding themselves our equals in all things. If they look back through this history to trace their connection with those days by blood, they find they have none… but when they look through that old Declaration of Independence, they find that those old men say that 'We hold these truths to be self-evident, that all men are created equal," and then they feel that that moral sentiment taught in that day evinces their relation to those men, that it is the father of all moral principle in them, and that they have a right to claim it as though they were blood of the blood, and flesh of the men who wrote that Declaration, and so they are." Abraham Lincoln, speech in Chicago, July 10, 1858.

175 "All this native land talk is nonsense. The native land of the American negro is America. His bones, his muscles, his sinews, are all American.

His ancestors for two hundred and seventy years have lived, and labored, and died on American soil." Frederick Douglass, "Lessons of the Hour" speech, Jan. 9, 1894.

176 "...let the poor, the needy, and oppressed of the earth... resort to the fertile plains of our western country, to the second land of promise, and there dwell in peace, fulfilling the first and great commandment." George Washington, letter to David Humphreys, July 25, 1785.

177 "Our principle in this matter should be absolutely simple. In the first place, we should insist that if the immigrant who comes here does in good faith become an American and assimilates himself to us, he shall be treated on an exact equality with everyone else, for it is an outrage to discriminate against any such man because of creed, or birthplace, or origin. But this is predicated upon the man's becoming in that very fact an American and nothing but an American. If he tries to keep segregated with men of his own origin and separated from the rest of America, then he isn't doing his part as an American. There can be no divided allegiance here." Theodore Roosevelt, letter to Richard Hurd, Jan. 3, 1919.

178 Those who seek asylum ought to declare their wish to do so at the border, not within it. Only in certain instances, such as when they are being closely pursued by those who mean to do them harm, ought exception to be granted.

179 The Constitution prohibits bills of attainder, which were once used in England to condemn the descendants of men convicted of crimes. "No Bill of Attainder or ex post facto Law shall be passed." Art. 1, Sec. 9; "... no Attainder of Treason shall work Corruption of Blood, or Forfeiture except during the Life of the Person attainted." Art. 3, Sec. 3.

180 "All persons born or naturalized in the United States, and subject to the jurisdiction thereof, are citizens of the United States and of the State wherein they reside." *U.S. Constitution*, 14th Amendment. The clause "subject to the jurisdiction thereof," which is the object of the current controversy, is meant to exclude only the children of foreign diplomats, who, as official representatives of their country, are immune to certain U.S. laws and thus are outside the jurisdiction of the United States.

181 The Immigration and Nationality Act currently permits issuance of 675,000 permanent residency visas per year. The President sets an additional quota for acceptance of refugees, which in 2019 stood at

30,000.

182 Under the Act above referenced, 480,000 immigrants are granted permanent residency out of family preference, 140,000 for reasons of employment, and 55,000 from the diversity visa lottery. This sum does not count refugees.

183 "For it's the great life force of each generation of new Americans that guarantees that America's triumph shall continue unsurpassed into the next century and beyond. Other countries may seek to compete with us; but in one vital area, as a beacon of freedom and opportunity that draws the people of the world, no country on Earth comes close." Ronald Reagan, remarks at the Presentation of the Presidential Medal of Freedom, Jan. 19, 1989.

184 "Those who plan for a city to make a great empire should contrive with all industry to make it full of inhabitants, for without this abundance of men one will never succeed in making a city great." Niccolò Machiavelli, *Discourses on Titus Livy*, Bk. 2, Ch. 3.

185 We presume, for instance, as a matter of good sense, that nobody intends to argue for committing federal funds towards fencing the wilderness of the Alaska-Yukon border. So ought it to be for other remote wildlands.

186 By which we refer to criminal offenses of a violent or otherwise grave nature; not, for instance, a traffic ticket.

187 Including, of course, our Republic's founding documents. Any translation, no matter how excellent, loses some of the original meaning; to read the Declaration of Independence and the Constitution in English is thus invaluable.

188 NATO meets this standard; its members are bound by the North Atlantic Treaty to come to each other's aid. Our Republic also has treaties to similar effect with Japan, South Korea, Australia, and the Philippines.

189 We do not, however, suggest that the government of the United States, pursuant to such a policy, ought to be able to revoke a person's U.S. citizenship without their consent. To do so, as mentioned above in connection to birthright citizenship, opens the door to tyrannical abuse. The prohibition placed on such an act by the 1967 Supreme Court decision in *Afroyim v. Rusk* is thus largely a good one: the evil wrought by enforcement must not exceed the good brought by a law or policy.

NO. 11 – ON FOREIGN POLICY

190 Here we distinguish might, which is a latent measure of power, from force, which we define as an act of coercion.

191 The Great Game in its narrow sense is the term given to the competition between Imperial Russia and Great Britain in Central Asia during the 19th century; but it can also be applied to great-power competition broadly, as we do here.

192 "If there were only small nations and no great ones, humanity would surely be freer and happier; but one cannot make it so that there are no great nations… Small nations are often miserable not because they are small, but because they are weak; great ones prosper not because they are great, but because they are strong. Force is therefore often one of the first conditions of happiness and even of existence of nations." Alexis de Tocqueville, *Democracy in America*, Vol. 1, Part 1, Ch. 8. Tocqueville here uses the term 'force' in the way that we have defined 'might.'

193 "Because it is impossible to foresee or define the extent and variety of national exigencies, or the correspondent extent and variety of the means which may be necessary to satisfy them." Alexander Hamilton, *Federalist No. 23*.

194 "It then could have been said to her, as it is now said to us, 'Why go beyond your own borders? Within them you have what suffices for your needs and those of your population. There are manifold abuses within to be corrected, manifold miseries to be relieved. Let the outside world take care of itself. Defend yourself, if attacked; being, however, always careful to postpone preparation to the extreme limit of imprudence. Sphere of influence, part in the world, national prestige – there are no such things; or if there be, they are not worth fighting for.' What England would have been, had she so reasoned, is matter for speculation; that the world would have been poorer may be confidently affirmed." Alfred Thayer Mahan, "The Isthmus and Sea Power," 1898.

195 "We have no eternal allies, and we have no perpetual enemies. Our interests are eternal and perpetual, and those interests it is our duty to follow." Lord Palmerston, speech to the House of Commons, Mar. 1, 1848.

196 Of the former: Britain, Canada, Australia, New Zealand, France, Germany, Japan, South Korea, India, Israel, and more. The latter: China, Russia, North Korea, Iran, and more. Some of the former are constitutional monarchies that are not republics in name, but have

republican institutions that uphold their liberty; whereas the latter claim to be republics, but are so in name only. It must also be clear that it has long been the policy of the United States to object only to foreign governments and never to their people, whom we assume to share a universal aspiration for liberty.

197 Indeed, our Republic often made such temporary arrangements with the Soviet Union.

198 As it did, for instance, in the Venezuelan Crisis of 1902-1903. Germany and Britain, to whom Venezuela owed a large sum of money, blockaded Caracas and threatened to seize Venezuelan territory, an outcome unacceptable to the United States. Theodore Roosevelt, President at the time, acted astutely to uphold U.S. interests. By assembling the U.S. Navy at Puerto Rico, he demonstrated might; with informal diplomacy, he conveyed the threat of force in secret to Germany, and also sowed division between London and Berlin; by referring the matter to formal arbitration at the International Court of Justice, he allowed Wilhelm II to save face. War was averted, and the blockade lifted.

199 "We see, therefore, that war is not merely an act of policy, but a true political instrument, a continuation of political intercourse carried on with other means. What remains peculiar to war is simply the peculiar nature of its means." Carl von Clausewitz, *On War*, Ch. 1, Sec. 24.

200 "Using words of little honor against the enemy arises most often from an insolence that either victory or the false hope of victory gives you. This false hope makes men err not only in speaking but also in working. For when this hope enters into the breasts of men, it makes them pass beyond the mark and most often lose the opportunity of having a certain good through hoping to have an uncertain better." Niccolò Machiavelli, *Discourses on Titus Livy*, Bk. 2, Ch. 27.

201 "To be prepared for war is one of the most effectual means of preserving peace. A free people ought not only to be armed, but disciplined; to which end a uniform and well-digested plan is requisite." George Washington, address to Congress, Jan. 8, 1790.

202 "I believe that one of the great prudences men use is to abstain from menacing or injuring anyone with words. For neither the one nor the other takes force away from the enemy, but the one makes him more cautious and the other makes him have greater hatred against you and think with greater industry of how to hurt you." Niccolò Machiavelli,

Discourses on Titus Livy, Bk. 2, Ch. 26.

203 Credibility does not require detailed specificity. It is unwise to telegraph the exact manner of a planned retaliation, for doing so would give the foe an opportunity to prepare countermeasures that could render the response impotent. Rather, our Republic ought to make known the general contours of its response to an anticipated challenge, enough that a rival may ponder the consequences of acting against our interest, but may not formulate a plan to thwart them.

204 "For one ought to accept this conclusion: that a captain who wishes to stay in the field cannot flee battle whenever the enemy wishes to engage it in any mode." Niccolò Machiavelli, *Discourses on Titus Livy*, Bk. 3, Ch. 10.

205 Thus, the failure to strike Syria in 2013 invited the Russian annexation of Crimea the following year. Our Union acted more astutely when the situation, regarding Syrian use of chemical weapons, recurred in 2018. In bombarding a Syrian airbase within days of that challenge, it acted promptly; by using force, it earned credibility; by using force proportionally and allowing Moscow to save face, it did not court escalation.

206 "China and Russia challenge American power, influence, and interests, attempting to erode American security and prosperity. They are determined to make economies less free and less fair, to grow their militaries, and to control information and data to repress their societies and expand their influence." U.S. National Security Strategy, 2017.

207 "Further, is it too much to say that, as two of these links, the shipping and the markets, are exterior to our own borders, the acknowledgement of them carries with it a view of the relations of the United States to the world radically distinct from the simple idea of self-sufficingness? We shall not follow far this line of thought before there will dawn the realization of America's unique position, facing the older worlds of the East and West, her shores washed by the oceans which touch the one or the other, but which are common to her alone." Alfred Thayer Mahan, "The United States Looking Outward," 1890.

208 Foreign trade is drawn naturally to the largest, most varied, and most open economies. As such, the greatest volumes of trade will either flow through the Pacific and Eurasia, with China at the center, or through the Pacific and the Atlantic, converging on the United States. In the 19th

century, Europe was the center, and both America and China stood on the periphery – as is still represented today on maps of the world.

209 Placing Nigeria on the now-notorious 'travel ban' list was a poor start, which shall serve only to increase Chinese influence there. A better investment, perhaps, would be to support the aspirations of those countries for reform of the United Nations Security Council, so as to reflect their growing role in the world.

210 "The central challenge to U.S. prosperity and security is the reemergence of long-term, strategic competition by what the National Security Strategy classifies as revisionist powers. It is increasingly clear that China and Russia want to shape a world consistent with their authoritarian model – gaining veto authority over other nations' economic, diplomatic, and security decisions." U.S. National Defense Strategy, 2018.

211 "Challenges to the U.S. military advantage represent another shift in the global security environment. For decades the United States has enjoyed uncontested or dominant superiority in every operating domain. We could generally deploy our forces when we wanted, assemble them where we wanted, and operate how we wanted. Today, every domain is contested – air, land, sea, space, and cyberspace." U.S. National Defense Strategy, 2018.

212 Such as the development of the F-35 fighter jet, which is expected to cost $1.5 trillion over the project's lifespan; yet it remains uncertain whether that aircraft could survive close combat against a swarm of inexpensive drones.

213 Of critical importance is that soldiers, sailors, airmen, and marines are trained exhaustively in basic tasks, and that they are trained also to perform those tasks without the aid of computers, which can be hacked or incapacitated. An infantryman who can use a map and compass can fight on when his GPS is jammed; an artilleryman who can fire using a chart can still attack the enemy when his fire control system dies. These abilities have been neglected of late in the U.S. military; it is unlikely that the Chinese and Russian militaries are neglecting them as well.

214 As coined and defined by the political scientist Joseph Nye.

215 The Department of Defense has now taken steps to accumulate a stockpile. These efforts ought to be continued.

216 This method has, of course, been made more difficult by the present administration's dishonorable abandonment of the Syrian Democratic

Forces, who bore the battle against ISIS. Yet credibility can recover over time and through the keeping of new promises. Our Republic ought now to begin laboring toward that end.

217 "Nations which went down fighting rose again, but those which tamely surrendered were finished." Winston Churchill, reply to Lord Halifax's demand in a Cabinet meeting to explore German terms, May 28, 1940. In his reply, Churchill echoed an ancient principle: "One other thing here is also very much to be esteemed, which is that one ought to wish to acquire glory even when losing; and one has more glory in being conquered by force than through another inconvenience that has made you lose." Niccolò Machiavelli, *Discourses on Titus Livy*, Bk. 3, Ch. 10.

218 "It was evident to my mind that the election of a Republican President in 1856 meant the secession of all the Slave States, and rebellion. Under these circumstances I preferred the success of a candidate whose election would prevent or postpone secession, to seeing the country plunged into a war the end of which no man could foretell. …I therefore voted for James Buchanan for President. Four years later the Republican party was successful in electing its candidate to the Presidency. The civilized world has learned the consequence. Four millions of human beings held as chattels have been liberated; the ballot has been given to them; the free schools of the country have been opened to their children." Ulysses S. Grant, *Personal Memoirs*, Ch. 16.

219 "Fondly do we hope, fervently do we pray, that this mighty scourge of war may speedily pass away. Yet, if God wills that it continue until all the wealth piled by the bondsman's two hundred and fifty years of unrequited toil shall be sunk, and until every drop of blood drawn with the lash shall be paid by another drawn with the sword, as was said three thousand years ago, so still it must be said, 'the judgments of the Lord are true and righteous altogether.'" Abraham Lincoln, Second Inaugural Address, Mar. 4, 1865.

NO. 12 – ON INTERNATIONAL COOPERATION

220 "It is a very true thing that all worldly things have a limit to their life… So those are better ordered and have a longer life that by means of their orders can often be renewed or indeed that through some accident outside the said order come to the said renewal. And it is a thing clearer than light that these bodies do not last if they do not renew themselves." Niccolò Machiavelli, *Discourses on Titus Livy*, Bk. 3, Ch. 1.

221 "I therefore maintain that since sovereignty is merely the exercise of the general will, it can never be alienated, and that the sovereign, which is only a collective being, cannot be represented by anything but itself. Power can perfectly well be transmitted, but not the will." Jean-Jacques Rousseau, *On the Social Contract*, Bk. 2, Ch. 1.

222 "He [the President] shall have Power, by and with the Advice and Consent of the Senate, to make Treaties, provided two thirds of the Senators present concur;" *U.S. Constitution*, Art. 2, Sec. 2; "This Constitution, and the laws of the United States which shall be made in Pursuance thereof; and all Treaties made, or which shall be made, under the Authority of the United States, shall be the supreme Law of the Land;" *U.S. Constitution*, Art. 6.

223 "There is nothing absurd or impracticable in the idea of a league or alliance between independent nations, for certain defined purposes precisely stated in a treaty; regulating all the details of time, place, circumstance, and quantity; leaving nothing to future discretion; and depending for its execution on the good faith of the parties. Compacts of this kind exist among all civilized nations subject to the usual vicissitudes of peace and war, of observance and nonobservance, as the interests or passions of the contracting powers dictate." Alexander Hamilton, *Federalist No. 15*.

224 This logic follows the non-delegation principle of legislative power that we examined in our essay on bureaucracy. Just as it is not necessarily sufficient that a regulation is pursuant to a law passed by Congress if it introduces new obligations on citizens, so it is not necessarily sufficient that an international decision is pursuant to a ratified treaty if it introduces new obligations on our Republic.

225 "In the early part of the present century, there was an epidemical rage in Europe for this species of compacts; from which the politicians of the times fondly hoped for benefits which were never realized. With a view to establishing the equilibrium of power and the peace of that part of the world, all the resources of negotiation were exhausted, and triple and quadruple alliances were formed; but they were scarcely formed before they were broken, giving an instructive but afflicting lesson to mankind on how little dependence is to be placed on treaties which have no other sanction than the obligations of good faith; and which oppose general considerations of peace and justice to the impulse of any immediate interest and passion." Alexander Hamilton, *Federalist No. 15*.

226 NATO has to some extent been an exception, due in part to the fact that it contains elements of a confederation.

227 "History furnishes no example of a free republic, anything like the extent of the United States. The Grecian republics were of small extent; so also was that of the Romans. Both of these, it is true, in process of time, extended their conquests over large territories of country; and the consequence was, that their governments were changed from that of free governments to those of the most tyrannical that ever existed in the world." 'Brutus,' *Letter No. 1.*

228 "The proposed Constitution therefore is in strictness neither a national nor a federal constitution; but a composition of both. In its foundation, it is federal, not national; in the sources from which the ordinary powers of the Government are drawn, it is partly federal and partly national; in the operation of these powers, it is national, not federal; in the extent of them again, it is federal, not national; and finally, in the authoritative mode of introducing amendments, it is neither wholly federal, nor wholly national." James Madison, *Federalist No. 39*. The Founders used 'federal' and 'confederate' interchangeably, as history had until then only furnished examples of the looser association which we here term a confederation. In framing a Constitution with the traits described by Madison, they created the form of association that we here refer to as a federation. The United States was the first such federation; and the distinction which grew thereafter between federation and confederation became clear when the secessionists of the Civil War referred to their government as 'confederate' and our Union's as 'federal.'

229 "The great and radical vice in the construction of the existing Confederation is the principle of legislation for states or governments, in their corporate or collective capacities and as contradistinguished from the individuals of whom they consist. ...The consequence of this is, that though in theory their resolutions concerning those objects are laws, constitutionally binding on the members of the Union, yet in practice they are mere recommendations, which the States observe or disregard at their option." Alexander Hamilton, *Federalist No. 15*. He refers to the Articles of Confederation, which provided a system of government for our Union so poor it had to be replaced within a decade by the federal Constitution. When it was again attempted by the rebel Confederate States, the same failings returned; thus, even had they not perpetuated the evil of slavery nor been at war with the legitimate government of the

Union, their endeavor would eventually have collapsed due to internal strife arising from the inadequacy of its constitution.

230 This is not to imply that the UN is altogether impotent, only that it is unequal to its stated purpose in Sec. 1, Art. 1 of its Charter: "to maintain international peace and security… to take effective collective measures for the prevention and removal of threats to the peace, and for the suppression of acts of aggression…" By that standard, the UN has proven ineffective. It has, however, done effective work as relates to its purpose in Sec. 3 of Art. 1, "…to achieve international co-operation in solving international problems of an economic, social, cultural, or humanitarian character…" mainly in the realm of preventing famine and disease. The UN is thus effective in accomplishing ends that all countries can agree upon – which are few, indeed, and inadequate to that institution's whole purpose. For its worth in that limited scope, however, and in providing a forum for consultation, it certainly ought to be preserved.

231 Thus has OPEC been an effective institution, despite counting among its members fierce strategic rivals.

232 "It is essential to the idea of a law, that it be attended with a sanction; or, in other words, a penalty or punishment for disobedience. If there be no penalty annexed to disobedience, the resolutions or commands which pretend to be laws will in fact amount to nothing more than advice or recommendation." Alexander Hamilton, *Federalist No. 15*.

233 The European Union has representative bodies, in the form of the European Parliament and the European Council, but those have been less vigorous than the bureaucratic European Commission; regulations produced by that body have raised the ire of European citizens and created an opening for the pernicious peddlers of 'illiberal democracy.'

234 It can exclude from its ventures a country that denies it the use of national facilities, which, given the prestige of exploration, is a strong incentive for members to cooperate. It is also entirely independent from the European Union.

235 Envision, for instance, a reconstituted Trans-Pacific Partnership or a North American Epidemic Response Center.

236 *The Economist* newspaper has used the term in relation to the European Union, among others.

237 "It is unlikely that the states that associate will be of the same size and

have equal power. The republic of the Lycians was an association of twenty-three towns; the large ones had three votes in the common council; the medium-sized ones, two; the small ones, one. ...The towns of Lycia paid the costs in proportion to their votes. ...If one had to propose a model of a fine federal republic, I would choose the republic of Lycia." Montesquieu, *Spirit of the Laws*, Bk. 9, Ch. 3. Montesquieu used the term 'federal' to refer to what we now consider a confederation. This consideration does not apply to federations today; as their constituent parts limit a greater part of sovereignty to the center and lack the right to exit the federation, their interests must be guarded by some equal representation.

238 Though this does not mean that cooperation with them on certain objects cannot prove fruitful.

239 Now the Commonwealth of Nations. Some of its members are constitutional monarchies, and not republics in name; but they share representative institutions.

240 "Confederations are broken for utility. In this, republics are by far more observant of accords than are princes. Examples could be brought up in which the least utility has made a prince break faith and a great utility has not made a republic break faith." Niccolò Machiavelli, *Discourses on Titus Livy*, Bk. 1, Ch. 59.

NO. 13 – ON GREAT WORKS

241 "One distinguishing characteristic of really civilized men is foresight; we have to, as a nation, exercise foresight for this nation in the future; and if we do not exercise that foresight, dark will be the future!" Theodore Roosevelt, opening address to the 1st Governors' Conference, May 13, 1908.

242 There are a thousand ways to imagine such an apocalyptic event. Yet one requires no speculation because it has already occurred: the meteor impact that brought an end to the dinosaurs, of whom nothing but bones remain.

243 "Every one, as he is bound to preserve himself, and not to quit his station willfully, so by the like reason, when his own preservation comes not into competition, ought he, as much as he can, to preserve the rest of mankind." John Locke, *Second Treatise of Government*, Ch. 2, Para. 6.

244 "But though this be a state of liberty, yet it is not a state of license: though

man in that state have an uncontroulable liberty to dispose of his person or possessions, yet he has not liberty to destroy himself, or so much as any creature in his possession, but where some nobler use than its bare preservation calls for it." John Locke, *Second Treatise of Government*, Ch. 2, Para. 6.

245 Under current law, the U.S. Army's largest exercises may grind to a halt if they encounter certain endangered species. This is absurd: the defense of the Republic is more important than the preservation of a woodpecker.

246 "Disregarding for the moment the question of moral purpose, it is safe to say that the prosperity of our people depends directly on the energy and intelligence with which our natural resources are used. It is equally clear that these resources are the final basis of national power and perpetuity. Finally, it is ominously evident that these resources are in the course of rapid exhaustion." Theodore Roosevelt, opening address to the 1st Governors' Conference.

247 "As a people we have the right and the duty, second to none other but the right and duty of obeying the moral law, of requiring and doing justice, to protect ourselves and our children against the wasteful development of our natural resources, whether that waste is caused by the actual destruction of such resources or by making them impossible of development hereafter." Theodore Roosevelt, opening address to the 1st Governors' Conference, May 13, 1908.

248 It is now referred to as climate change; that there may be scientific reasons for this change in nomenclature, we do not dispute. But this is a political essay, not a scientific one. We find global warming to be clearer and more vivid: it cuts to the problem's core, the inexorable rise in temperature, and conveys its worldwide character. It is also less tainted by partisan rancor. Both parties once feared global warming; only one now worries about climate change.

249 "We want to take action that will prevent the advent of a woodless age, and defer as long as possible the advent of an ironless age." Theodore Roosevelt, opening address to the 1st Governors' Conference, May 13, 1908.

250 The present administration has, rightly, again made exploration of the Moon and Mars into a formal objective.

251 That the Moon has no atmosphere and less gravity than the Earth might

also make it a more efficient launchpad for expeditions deeper into the solar system and beyond.

252 Clean being defined herein as emitting less carbon dioxide. Natural gas has promise; cleaner than oil and coal, it is becoming less expensive to produce. Such is also the case with wind and solar power, but only where the climate is advantageous: it might make good economic sense to maintain solar panels near Tucson, but not around Seattle.

253 It need hardly be said that at the moment an extraordinary need for research funds is presented by the COVID-19 pandemic, which is of more immediate importance than the two matters referred to here.

254 Well-defined suggestions for a carbon tax have been put forth by *The Economist* newspaper, among others.

255 "There will be, as there always are, pressures in this country to do less in this area as in so many others, and temptations to do something else that is perhaps easier. But this research here must go on. This space effort must go on. The conquest of space must and will go ahead. That much we know. That much we can say with confidence and conviction." John F. Kennedy, remarks at the Aerospace Medical Health Center, Nov. 21, 1963.

256 For AI to control electronic weapons, such as signal jammers, that can only harm other machines, is acceptable.

257 Such as for severe genetic disorders or cancers that do not respond to other treatment. The use of gene-altering technologies on crops is another matter. It is indispensable to feeding the present world population of seven billion; and by increasing the crop yield per acre of land, it supports the aim of conservation.

258 "Frank O'Connor, the Irish writer, tells in one of his books how, as a boy, he and his friends would make their way across the countryside, and when they came to an orchard wall that seemed too high and too doubtful to try and too difficult to permit their voyage to continue, they took off their hats and tossed them over the wall – and then they had no choice but to follow them. This Nation has tossed its cap over the wall of space, and we have no choice but to follow it. Whatever the difficulties, they will be overcome. Whatever the hazards, they must be guarded against. ...with the help and support of all Americans, we will climb this wall with safety and with speed – and we shall then explore the wonders on the other side." John F. Kennedy, remarks at the Aerospace Medical

Health Center, Nov. 21, 1963.

259 "Finally, let us remember that the conservation of our natural resources, though the gravest problem of today, is yet but part of another and greater problem to which this Nation is not yet awake, but to which it will awake in time, and with which it must hereafter grapple if it is to live – the problem of national efficiency, the patriotic duty of insuring the safety and continuance of the Nation. When the People of the United States consciously undertake to raise themselves as citizens, and the Nation and the States in their several spheres, to the highest pitch of excellence in private, State, and national life, and to do this because it is the first of all duties of true patriotism, then and not till then the future of this Nation, in quality and in time, will be assured." Theodore Roosevelt, opening address to the 1st Governors' Conference, May 13, 1908.

THE PAST, THE PRESENT, AND THE FUTURE

260 "These considerations speak a persuasive language to every reflecting and virtuous mind, and exhibit the continuance of the Union as a primary object of Patriotic desire. Is there a doubt, whether a common government can embrace so large a sphere? Let experience solve it. ... We are authorized to hope that a proper organization of the whole, with the auxiliary agency of governments for the respective Sub divisions, will afford a happy issue to the experiment. 'Tis well worth a fair and full experiment." George Washington, Farewell Address, September 17, 1796.

261 "You give me a credit to which I have no claim, in calling me 'the writer of the Constitution of the U.S.' This was not, like the fabled Goddess of Wisdom, the offspring of a single brain. It ought to be regarded as the work of many heads and many hands." James Madison, in a letter to William Cogswell, March 10, 1834.

AFTERWORD

262 Such as when Marius was awarded four consecutive consulships when the Cimbri and the Teutones appeared to menace Italy.

263 The Social War, from 91-87 B.C.

BIBLIOGRAPHY

264 When I have referred to content that is not in the public domain, such

as recent news articles, I have cited the source in the applicable endnote.

Made in United States
North Haven, CT
05 June 2023